D1785157

Horse Riding For Beginners

Vicki Rickabaugh
ILLUSTRATIONS BY JILL BENEDICT

Photos by Vincent Serbin.

Distributed in the UNITED STATES by T.F.H. Publications, Inc., 211 West Sylvania Avenue, Neptune City, NJ 07753; in CANADA by H & L Pet Supplies Inc., 27 Kingston Crescent, Kitchener, Ontario N2B 2T6; Rolf C. Hagen Ltd., 3225 Sartelon Street, Montreal 382 Quebec; in ENGLAND by T.F.H. Publications Limited, 4 Kier Park, Ascot, Berkshire SL5 7DS; in AUSTRALIA AND THE SOUTH PACIFIC by T.F.H. (Australia) Pty. Ltd., Box 149, Brookvale 2100 N.S.W., Australia; in NEW ZEALAND by Ross Haines & Son, Ltd., 18 Monmouth Street, Grey Lynn, Auckland 2 New Zealand; in SINGAPORE AND MALAYSIA by MPH Distributors (S) Pte., Ltd., 601 Sims Drive, # 03/07/21, Singapore 1438; in the PHILIPPINES by Bio-Research, 5 Lippay Street, San Lorenzo Village, Makati Rizal; in SOUTH AFRICA by Multipet Pty. Ltd., 30 Turners Avenue, Durban 4001. Published by T.F.H. Publications Inc. Manufactured in the United States of America by T.F.H. Publications, Inc.

Contents

A good grounding in the techniques of dressage will be of benefit whether you attempt some of the relatively more involved maneuvers such as jumping (above) or stick with simple non-jumping horsemanship.

ACKNOWLEDGMENTS

I WOULD LIKE TO EXPRESS MY DEEPEST GRATITUDE TO MY HUSBAND, RICK, FOR HIS CONTINUING UNDERSTANDING AND PATIENCE. TO THE MEMORY OF MAJOR DEZSO SZILAGYI FOR HIS VAST KNOWLEDGE, AND TO ALL MY STUDENTS FOR THEIR SUPPORT.

FOREWORD

Riding is an art, and the horse and rider are the artist. At any level and for whatever purpose, dressage can produce the kind of horse that is enjoyable to ride and a pleasure to watch. With proper development, dressage will allow the horse to move with all of his natural grace and freedom while under the control and influence of the rider's aids.

Dressage is a French word meaning "schooling" and when schooled in a systematic and methodical training program, the horse will become supple, relaxed and obedient. The training of the horse and rider can only come with knowledge, time, practice, and patience. When the horse and rider develop mentally and physically, riding will be a joy and the horse and rider will act as one.

It is the purpose of this book to explain and develop a basic teaching and training program to create harmony between the horse and rider.

Introduction

The horse, as we know it today, is a warm-blooded mammal that evolved from the group of mammals known as the *Eohippus*. The Eohippus lived over fifty million years ago. They had four toes on the front feet and three toes on the hind feet. From the Eohippus evolved the *Mesohippus,* which had three toes. Then came the *Merychippus,* followed by the one-toed *Pliohippus* and finally *Equus,* the modern horse. All members of the horse family have basically the same shape and body. Donkeys and Zebras are the horse's closest relatives.

Today there are numerous different groups and breeds of domestic horses. One method of classification is according to blood. A horse may be termed "hot-blooded," "warm-blooded" or "cold-blooded." The term "hot-blooded" does not refer to temperature but to horses like the Thoroughbred and Arab that are possessed of characteristics synonymous with refinement, speed and endurance. The term "cold-blooded" refers to heavier draft horses which are more attuned to cold weather and hard work. Warm blood is the mixture of the hot and cold breeds, resulting in a moderate, all-purpose breed.

Color

Horses come in a rainbow of colors. Black, when it occurs, generally covers the entire body, coat, mane and tail. A black horse occasionally has white markings on his face and legs.

A Bay is brown in color with a black mane, tail and legs. Chestnuts are also browns, but usually occur in different degrees of intensity of brown. The mane and tail of a Chestnut may be brown but some may have flaxen mane and tail.

Grays are covered with black and white hair throughout the

Every six to eight weeks the blacksmith should come and examine the horse's feet. The blacksmith will shape and trim the horse's feet and put shoes on the horse if the owner so desires.

Above: When first learning to lunge the horse or when lungeing a "green" horse, you may want an assistant either to help lead the horse on the circle or to help coordinate the aids of the lunge line and lunge whip on the circle. **Below:** Additional lungeing equipment, includes lungeing caveson, lunge line, lunge whip, and "side rein."

body and have black skin. With increasing age the coat grows lighter in color and may appear white.

A Dun-colored horse is further classified under different colors. One classification is called "blue dun" which is a deep black coloring that gives the appearance of blue. The blue dun horse may or may not have a black dorsal stripe. The other dun classification is a yellow dun. This is a yellow horse with black skin that also may or may not have a dorsal stripe.

A Palomino, although considered to be a type of breed, is also a color in which the horse is golden with a white mane and tail. The body is unmarked by any other color, except it may have white on its face and legs.

A Piebald is a horse covered with irregular black patches on white hair. Skewbald is a horse covered with brown or other colored patches, other than black on white. Spotted refers to horses possessing circular patches of hair in varying sizes that are not the same color as the general body.

Height and Gender

You will find that when it comes to horses, people have different tastes. Some people like grays and some like chestnuts. Some like their horses small and some large. The average height of a mature horse is 15.2, which means fifteen hands and two inches. The horse's height is measured from the withers to the ground level. A hand is equivalent to four inches; therefore a horse that is 15.2 would be 62 inches (15 hands x 4 inches plus 2 inches.)

At about three years of age the horse is old enough to start his schooling. When a horse is first born it is called a "foal." A male foal is a "colt" and a female foal is a "filly." When the colt becomes three years old it is then called a stallion. A castrated stallion at any age is called a gelding and an adult filly is called a mare. Most of the riding horses are either geldings or mares, but whether the horse of your choice is a stallion, gelding, or mare, to reach its optimum height and weight and stay healthy, good nutrition and proper exercise are necessary.

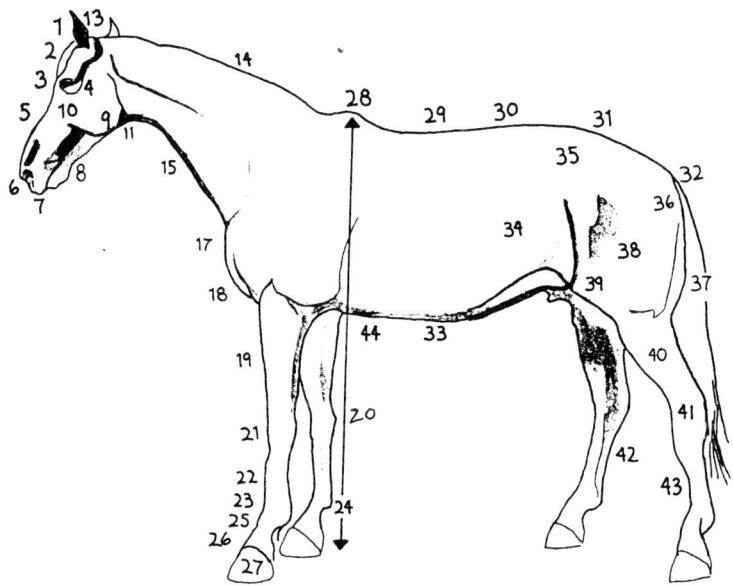

The parts of a horse. 1) Ear; 2) Forelock; 3) Forehead; 4) Eye; 5) Face; 6) Muzzle; 7) Mouth; 8) Chin groove; 9) Jowl; 10) Cheek; 11) Throat latch; 12) Jugular area; 13) Poll; 14) Mane and crest; 15) Neck; 16) Shoulder; 17) Point of shoulder; 18) Breast; 19) Forearm; 20) Elbow; 21) Knee; 22) Cannon bone; 23) Fetlock; 24) Height to withers; 25) Pastern; 26) Coronet; 27) Hoof; 28) Withers; 29) Back; 30) Loin; 31) Rump; 32) Dock; 33) Belly; 34) Flank; 35) Croup; 36) Point of buttocks; 37) Tail; 38) Thigh; 39) Stifle; 40) Gaskin; 41) Hock; 42) Chestnut; 43) Cannon bone.

Food and Feeding

The horse is fed two or three times a day. This is done because the horse's stomach is relatively small for its size, therefore feeding it small, frequent meals will help the horse's digestion. Much of the horse's nutrition comes from grain or hay. A horse may eat oats, corn, bran or "sweet feed," the last being a mixture of oats, corn and molasses. Along with eating grain, a horse will eat hay. Some of the more popular hays in order of their protein and nutritional value are grass, timothy, clover and alfalfa.

A cavalletti is described as a low, movable rail or pole. It should be eight to twelve feet long and four to twelve inches high.

Facing page: The main objective for working over cavalletti is to improve the horse's balance, suppleness, impulse, and rhythm.

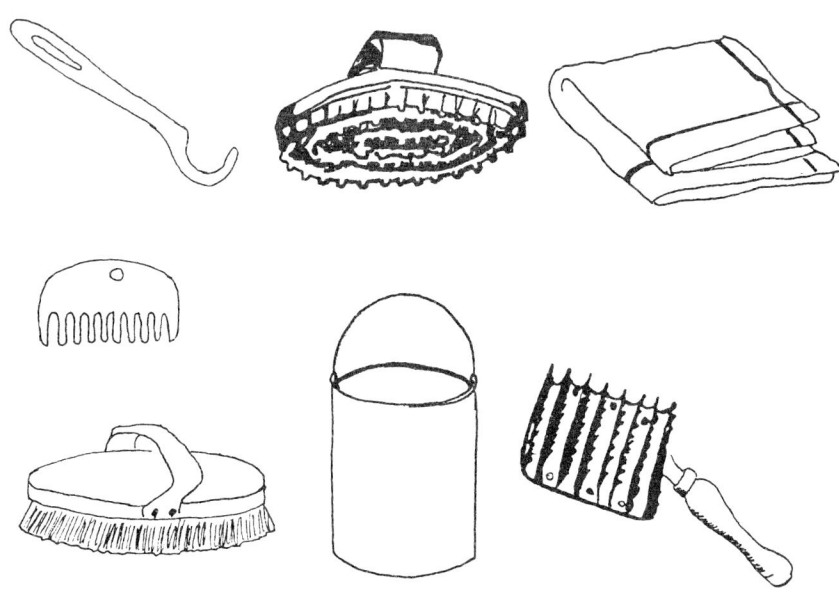
Grooming equipment

As a rule of thumb, between 1½ to 2 pounds of grain per hundred pounds of body weight in addition to about one pound of hay per hundred pounds of body weight should be fed to the horse daily. When discussing feed, it should be stressed that each horse is different and requires different amounts of feed to keep him looking good. The final decision of how much to feed a horse will be based on the quality of feed, the weight at which the horse looks best and the amount of exercise the animal is getting.

It is important to remember that grain must be stored in a safe place, as horses will over-eat if too much grain is made available. Horses also drink plenty of water, but you should never give water to an over-heated horse. Good feed and a good feeding program are the first steps to good horsemanship.

Grooming

The second step to good horsemanship is grooming. Thorough, regular grooming and cleanliness are essentials for the horse. Vigorous brushing stimulates circulation to the skin and muscles, improves the animal's appearance and contributes to its well-being and general health.

A horse should be groomed at least once a day. Some of the grooming equipment necessary for the horse's care are as follows: rubber curry comb; spring steel curry comb; mane comb; body brush; sweat scraper; sponges; and hoof pick.

The horse is groomed from head to hoof. The grooming may be done in a stall or on cross-ties. First, standing alongside the horse with curry comb in hand, rub the horse hair in a circular motion. This allows the dry sweat and dirt to loosen from the skin and also provides the horse with a good body massage. Curry combs should be used only on well-muscled areas of the horse. They should not be used on those parts of the body where the bones are directly under the skin, like the face or legs. Some horses have sensitive areas and may become ticklish while being groomed. Don't get alarmed—just brush more gently.

After the horse is "curried," it is brushed with the body brush. The body brush is an oval or oblong shaped brush with short, sturdy or soft bristles. Long firm strokes are used to remove all loose dirt from all parts of the horse's body. When the horse is finished being brushed be sure to check under the belly for any missed dirt. This will prevent girth sores from occurring. After a few brush strokes, take the curry comb and pass it through the brush. This will remove the dust and hair from the brush.

Another piece of grooming equipment is the mane comb. The mane comb comes in different sizes and is composed of aluminum or plastic. The comb is used on the horse's mane and forelock, but not the tail. The tail should be untangled by hand. While you are grooming the tail, stand to the side of the horse, never directly behind, because there is always a chance the horse may get frightened and kick out.

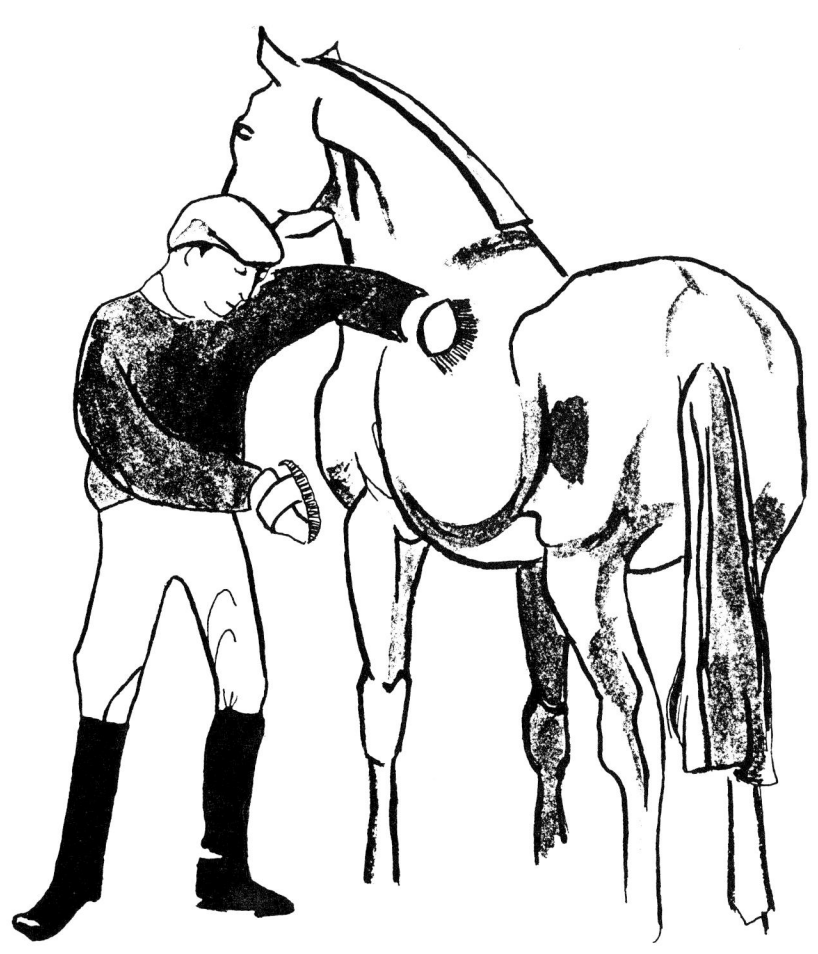

Cleaning the horse

Overleaf Facing page:
Posture and seat of rider. When looking at the rider from the side, the instructor should be able to draw an imaginary line through the shoulder, hip, and heel.

Overleaf:
A secure seat is achieved by lots of practice and patience. Riding without stirrups is an excellent way to improve the rider's position.

Cleaning the foot

Every part of the horse gets cleaned, including the horse's hooves. The horse's hooves should be cleaned at least once a day. Using a hoof pick, clean the hooves before taking him out of the stables. Relax; it is not difficult when you know how. First, stand next to the horse, facing towards the rear of the animal. Before bending over to raise the leg and hoof, stroke the shoulder and entire leg of the horse. This will alert the horse so that he will not be frightened. Next, prop the hoof on your knee so you can clean its lower surface. All the dirt, hay and manure on the lower surface of all four feet should be cleaned out. Remember, "no feet, no horse."

Every six to eight weeks the blacksmith should come and examine the horse's feet. The blacksmith will shape and trim the horse's feet and put shoes on the horse if the owner so desires. Properly trimmed feet will help prevent the horse from getting potentially crippling foot disorders.

To add the finishing touches to the horse's grooming, take the sponge and carefully wipe out its eyes and nostrils. The horse is now ready to be saddled and bridled.

The purpose of lungeing the rider is to teach him to maintain a balanced seat while the horse is in motion.

Facing page: Lungeing the rider is an ideal way to develop a rider's confidence, relaxation, and knowledge.

Equipment

Parts of the Saddle

The saddle is designed to give comfort to the horse and comfort and security to the rider. A saddle must fit the horse perfectly. Only in this way can pressure sores, tension in the back and general discomfort be avoided. The purpose of training a horse is to get the horse well balanced, supple, relaxed and obedient. An improperly fitting saddle or bridle will hinder this training program.

There are three major types of English saddles: "dressage," "all-purpose" and "jumping." Each of these saddles is designed in a special way to aid the rider's seat when jumping or when riding dressage. The major noticeable difference between the saddles is the position of the side panels. When looking at the different types of saddles you will readily be able to notice the difference between the jumping and the dressage saddle. The jumping saddle is designed in such a way that the side panels are set forward and the knee rolls are well padded. The forward placement of the panels will help the rider support himself when jumping. In contrast with the forward panels of the jumping saddle, the dressage saddle has straight panels with little padding in the knee rolls. When riding dressage the rider will use a longer stirrup length and will not need the kind of knee support as when jumping. The all-purpose saddle is the "middle of the road" model. The side panels are neither too far forward nor too straight. This saddle is used when the rider wants to do both jumping and dressage.

Underneath the saddle is placed a "saddle pad" which is made of felt, sheepskin or other absorbent material. It should be well-fitted to the underside of the saddle so that it will help absorb sweat and prevent irritation to the horse's back.

To secure the saddle on the horse's back a "girth" will be attached to the leather straps, called "billets," which can be found

DIFFERENT TYPES OF SADDLES

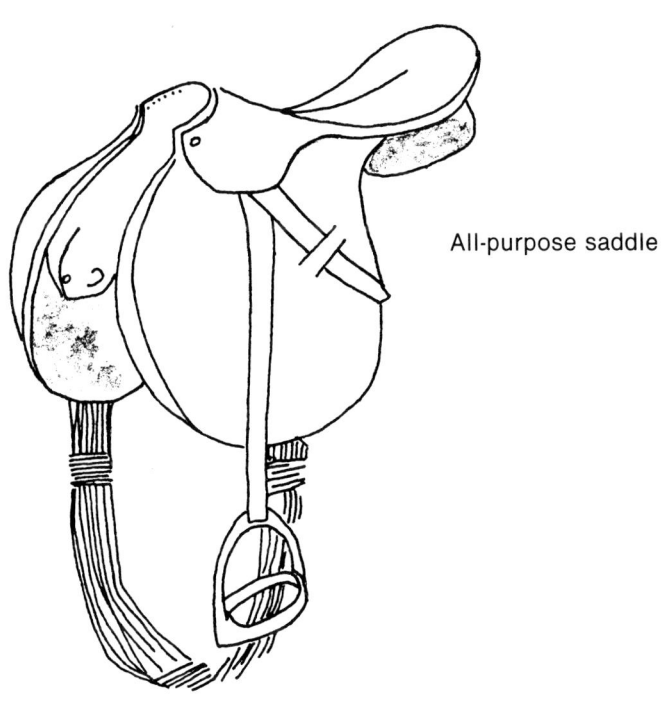

All-purpose saddle

Dressage saddle

Jumping saddle

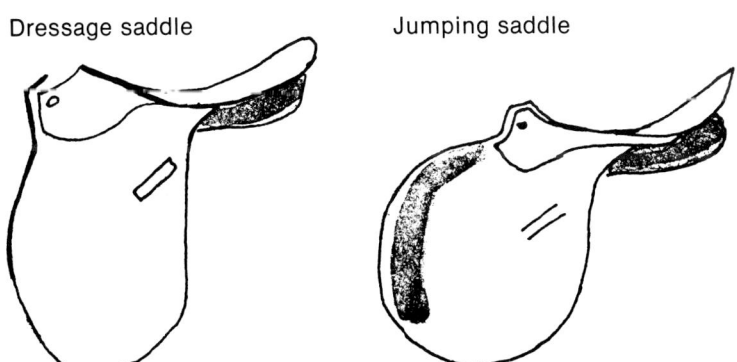

To aid in relaxation, control, and independence, certain following exercises can be carried out on the lunge line while the rider is sitting in the saddle. The exercises shown above and below are for the development of the waist and legs.

The exercise shown here is beneficial if the rider's shoulders and back are stiff.

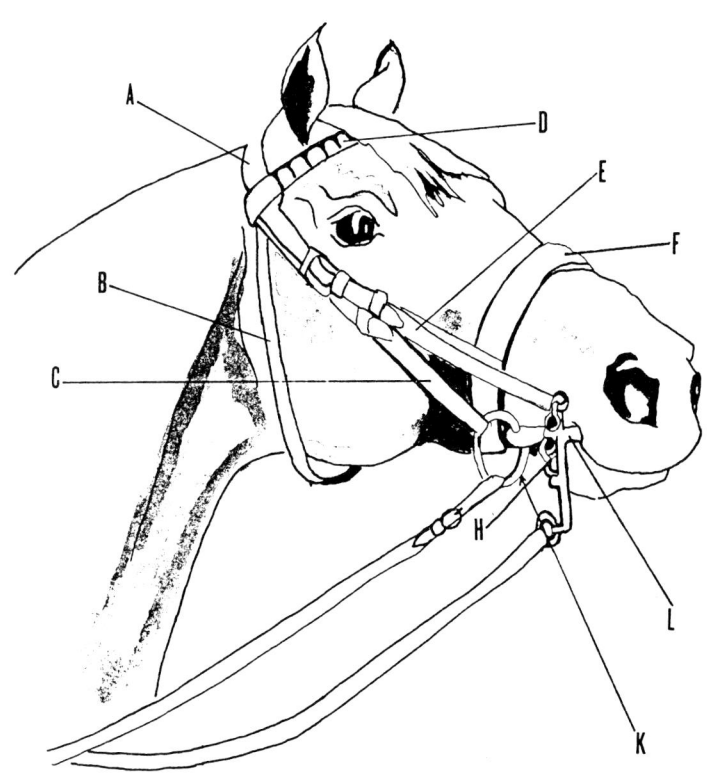

Parts of a double bridle. A) Headpiece; B) Throat latch; C) Cheek piece of snaffle; D) Brow band; E) Cheek piece of curb; F) Cavesson; G) Rein of snaffle; H) Curb chain; I) Rein of curb; K) Snaffle bit; L) Curb bit.

under the flaps of the saddle. A girth can be made of leather, cotton or nylon. The nylon girth has a greater tendency to rub or irritate the horse's skin, whereas the leather or cotton girths are softer and less likely to do so. Whatever girth you use on a horse, it and all horse equipment should be cleaned daily.

Parts of the Bridle

For regular training the bridle used for most horses is a simple bridle with snaffle bit, drop noseband or caveson noseband and one set of reins. A simple snaffle bit is preferred because it is a very mild bit and will not hurt the horse's mouth. The

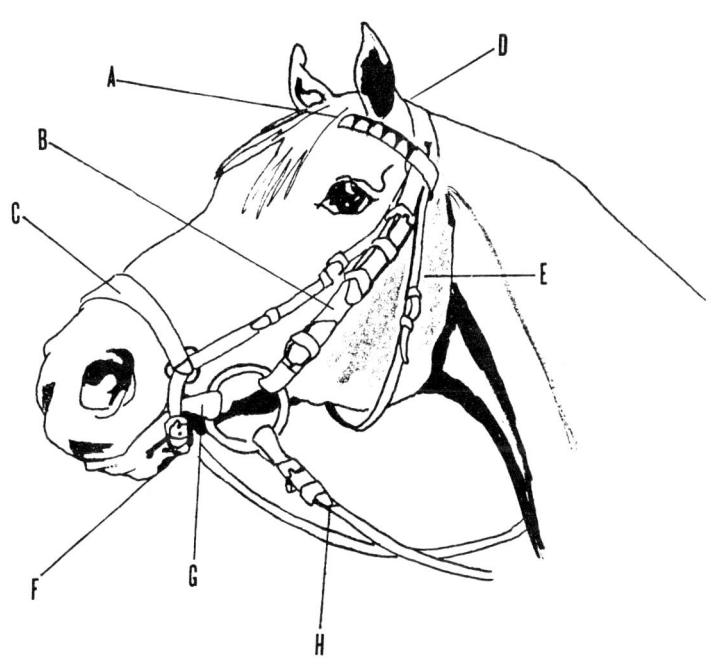

Parts of a snaffle bridle. A) Brow band; B) Cheek pieces; C) Cavesson or noseband; D) Headpiece; E) Throat latch; F) Chin strap; G) Snaffle bit; H) Rein.

bit will be attached to the leather cheek pieces and should be pulled up and adjusted so that there is not more than one wrinkle in the corners of the horse's mouth.

The double bridle should be used only by advanced riders with well educated horses. Because the double bridle has a snaffle bit and also consists of a curb bit with curb chain it can cause damage to the horse's mouth. For this reason only riders with educated and quiet hands and developed seats should use this bridle.

Now that you have an understanding of what the saddle and bridle are, the next step is to learn how to put the equipment on the horse.

A demonstration of riding the corner.

Facing page: At the halt the horse should be standing on all four legs, with the weight of the legs evenly distributed beneath it.

How to Saddle and Bridle Your Horse

Saddling and bridling your horse may be done either in the box stall or on cross-ties. Cross-ties are rope, nylon or chain restraints that are snapped on each side of the horse's halter and then secured to another point four to five feet away from the horse. A halter is a nylon or leather headstall that fits over the horse's head.

But before you go into the stall you must get the attention of the horse. When entering the stall, call out to the horse first and then enter the stall, walking on its left side. Each horse should have his own halter. Snap the lead line to the under ring of the halter and while standing on the left side of the horse lead the horse out of the stall and onto cross-ties. If the horse is not put on cross-ties but is tied to a post, be sure that the animal is tied only with a slip knot; that way, in case of an emergency, the horse can be freed quickly.

When you are putting the saddle and bridle on the horse, try not to be nervous. Remember, "practice makes perfect." With the bridle, saddle, girth and saddle pad on your left arm, step to the left of your horse and place the saddle pad and then the saddle on the horse's back, up by his withers. Then slide the saddle slightly to the rear of the horse so that the hairs on the back of the horse lie flat. Next, fasten the girth to the saddle. Be sure when fastening the girth to the saddle that the girth is flat and not twisted. Also be sure to allow at least one hand's width between the front leg and the girth. If the space between the girth and leg is too great, the saddle may be too far back. This too can give the horse a sore back and make riding difficult. If the space of the girth is too close to the front legs, the girth may pinch the skin and restrict the horse's movement.

The rider should always check the saddle and tighten the girth before getting on the horse. This is done to make sure the saddle is secure and won't slip off the horse while you are riding.

Once the saddle is securely on the horse, the rider can begin to bridle him. However, before you attempt to bridle the horse, first review all of the parts of the bridle. Having identified the

One method of putting the bridle on the horse.

parts of the bridle, place it in your left hand and position yourself parallel to the horse, facing toward the horse's head. With your right hand, place the reins over the horse's head and allow them to rest on the horse's neck. Next, using both hands, but without letting go of the bridle, unstrap the cross-ties and remove the halter from the horse. Be careful, because once the horse is off the cross-ties he may want to walk away. If this happens, just take hold of the reins that are around the horse's neck and say "whoa."

With your right hand, grasp the crown piece of the headstall and pull the crown piece over the horse's ears; at the same time, with your left hand, palm open, push the bit between the horse's teeth into the mouth. Please don't put your hand into the horse's mouth as you may get bitten.

The position of horse and rider near the beginning of the operation of making the circle. Note the rider's relaxed posture.

Another method of putting the bridle on the horse.

After the headstall is on and the bit is in the horse's mouth, if the bridle has a drop noseband, buckle it around the horse's muzzle. The muzzle is approximately four fingers above the nostrils. If the bridle has a caveson noseband, it will be buckled and adjusted to fit approximately two fingers below the cheek bones. The deciding factor for using a drop noseband or caveson noseband will depend upon the acceptance by the horse with the bit. If the horse constantly opens his mouth every time the rein aids are given, then the drop noseband will be used to keep the mouth closed. The last thing to be adjusted is the throat-latch. When buckling and adjusting the throat-latch there should be enough space for a fist to fit between the leather and the throat of the horse.

Check list 1. The ears and forelock stick out between the crown piece and brow-band. 2. The bit does not form more than one wrinkle on the sides of the mouth. 3. The drop noseband forms a ring around the horse's muzzle below the bit. If it is a caveson noseband it should form a ring above the bit. 4. The throat-latch is not too tightly buckled. 5. Lastly, smile, you have done a good job!

Remember, at first saddling and bridling a horse may seem complicated, but don't despair; with practice and patience it will become easy.

Rider's Equipment

Now that the horse is well groomed, all "tacked-up" and waiting to be led from the stable, let's take a moment and discuss proper grooming and attire for the rider. Whether you are just starting to ride or have been riding seriously for years, it is important that the clothing you wear be comfortable. For daily riding a shirt, sweater and riding breeches with boots are considered suitable attire. Breeches are form-fitting pants made of sturdy stretch fabirc and come in many different colors. As with all riding apparel, breeches may be bought right off the rack or can be custom made.

Whether you are purchasing breeches, a riding coat, hard hat or boots, everything should fit comfortably, especially your riding boots. Nothing is more upsetting than to ride for an hour or two in boots that are too tight. Riding boots are made of leather or rubber material. (Rubber boots are easier to maintain and usually cheaper.) Your riding boots should fit comfortably in the foot and extend up the lower leg, almost to the bend of the knee.

Also popular and acceptable among riding enthusiasts are "chaps." Chaps are a form of riding pants that are made of leather and zipped over the ordinary pants. Chaps protect the rider's legs and allow the rider's seat to grip the saddle better. Proper riding clothes help form a better bond between saddle and rider, which will ultimately enhance the riding of the horse.

34

The horse's equipment should always fit well and be at least as clean as the rider's personal equipment. Make sure that your shirt tails are tucked in, buttons are fastened, boots are cleaned and long hair is tied back. You are now ready to lead the horse out of the stable.

Leading the Horse

Before you lead the horse out of the stable take the riding reins that are around the horse's neck and place them over the horse's head into your hands. Next, stand on the left side of the horse, near the horse's neck or shoulder and with your right hand hold the reins just below the animal's chin. With your left hand, hold the riding reins near the buckle.

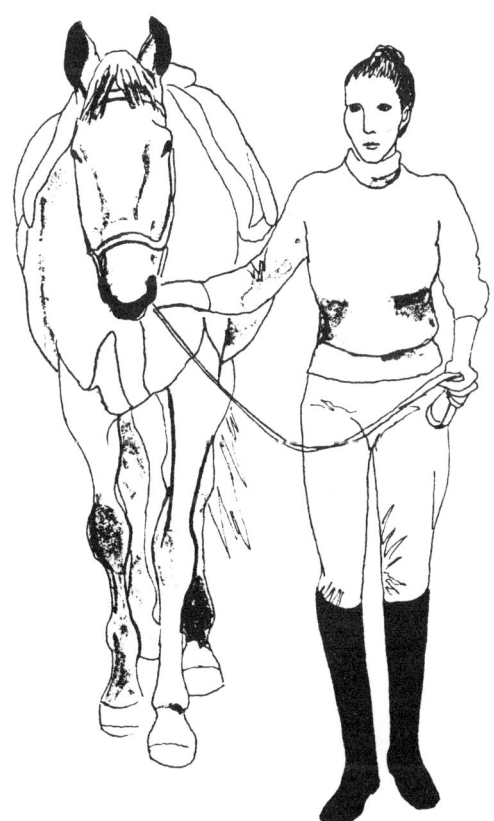

Leading the horse

It is important to remember when leading your horse that the stirrup irons should be tucked up in the stirrup-leathers. If they are hanging alongside the saddle they may get caught in something or they can hit the horse as he walks and frighten him. When leading your horse always look at where you are going and where you want to be. If the horse should stop, don't get alarmed; just urge him forward with your voice.

The horse and rider must have each other's confidence. Only then can the horse and rider progress. They are partners and they must have knowledge, understanding and time together, in order for the partnership to grow.

The collected walk.

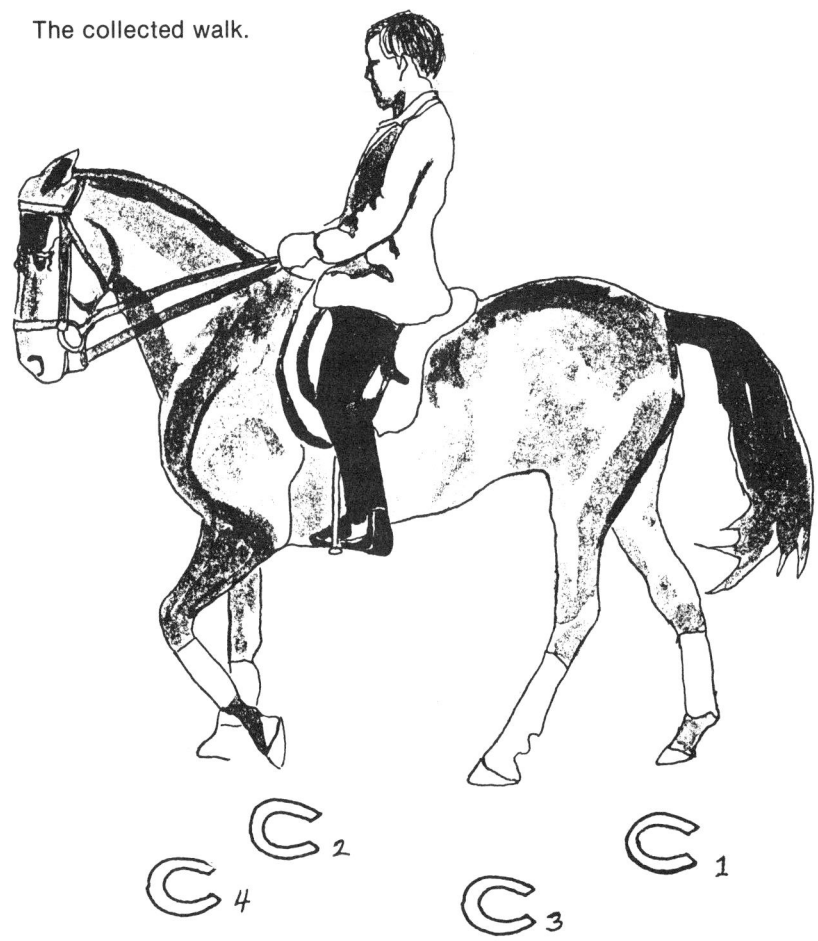

Training the Horse and Rider

Gaits

In the first stage of training, the horse is taught to go forward in good rhythm at the walk, trot and canter. The walk, trot and canter are called the horse's gaits. Within these gaits the tempo may be lengthened or shortened but always kept even and regular.

WALK: The walk is a pace of "four-time." This means that the horse moves his legs one after the other so that the rider will be able to hear all four hoof beats. The sequence of the horse's legs at the walk will be as follows: 1) Near hind; 2) Near fore; 3) Off hind; 4) Off fore. "Near hind" and "near fore" refer to the hind or front leg closest to the inside of the working area and "off hind" and "off fore" refer to the legs that are furthest or on the outside of the working area. When the horse is walking there are always two or three feet on the ground at the same time.

The different tempos of the walk are described as the "medium walk," "collected walk," "extended walk," and the "free walk." Whatever tempo of the gait the horse is exhibiting, the leg movement will always be in the same order.

TROT: The trot is a pace of "two-time." This means that each diagonal pair of legs will move alternately so that the rider will be able to hear two hoof beats. The seqence of the horse's legs at the trot will be: "off hind" and "near fore" together and then the "near hind" and "off fore" together. The different tempos of the trot are described as the "working trot," "medium trot," "extended trot," and "collected."

The collected trot.

CANTER: The canter is a pace of "three-time." This means that three beats will be heard by the rider. The sequence of the horse's legs at the canter will be: 1) "off hind," 2) "off fore" and "near hind" and 3) "near fore." The third beat of the canter is the leading leg. If the horse is cantering to the left, the third beat of the canter will be the left front leg. Therefore, the rider will say that the horse is going on the "left lead." When cantering to the right, the third beat of the canter will be the right front leg. This will be called the "right lead." The different tempos of the canter are described as the "working canter," "medium canter," and the "extended canter."

Remember, when riding the gaits or the different tempos within the gaits, the horse must maintain its forward rhythm.

The canter.

Starting the Training

It is very important that the rider set short range and long range goals for the horse and himself. Both horse and rider must develop mentally as well as physically.

Having led the horse out of the stable, lead him to the schooling area. At first, when learning to ride or "school" a horse, it is advisable to use an enclosed area that is free from obstacles. The use of an enclosed area will help eliminate some of the schooling problems that may be encountered when training the horse.

One of the best ways to establish confidence in the horse and set a good foundation for relaxation and obedience is by "lungeing." Lungeing is also helpful in exercising and developing the horse's muscles and it is also very beneficial in developing the rider's seat.

Lungeing the Horse

With an understanding of the horse's gaits, the rider can now start to lunge the horse. Lungeing is not a substitute for riding, but it is an important stepping stone in the foundation of schooling the horse and rider. When first learning to lunge the horse or when lungeing a "green" horse, you may want an assistant either to help lead the horse on the circle or to help coordinate the aids of the lunge line and lunge whip on the circle.

When lungeing, the trainer (rider) stands in the center of a circle and places himself near the horse's inside hip. With the aid of his voice and lunge whip he encourages the horse to move forward at the walk. When the horse moves off at the walk or any other gait, the movement and engagement will always start from the hindquarters. Only when the hindquarters are developed properly can the horse move forward correctly into the bit.

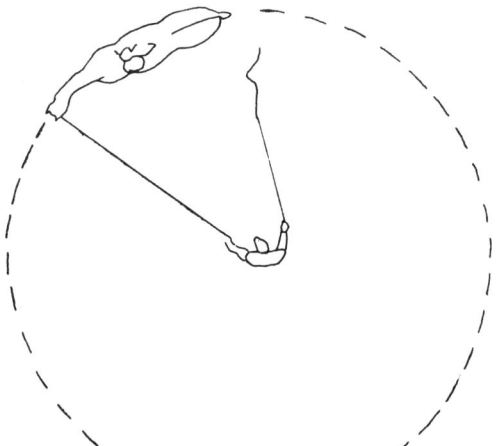

Standing position while lungeing

When the trainer wants the horse to slow down, or make a transition into another gait, the trainer shortens the lunge line, gives a voice command, and places himself near the shoulder of the horse. Eventually, with patience and practice the rider will be able to instruct the horse to walk, trot, canter and halt in any sequence on the lunge line.

It is important to remember during these exercises not to overwork the horse on the circle or make the circles too small. More harm than good can come from that type of training. Training the horse and rider is very similar; there must be short and long range goals set for each. Knowledge with confidence must come first when riding or working with horses.

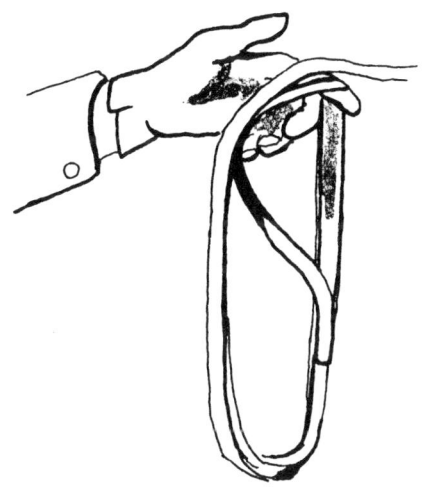

Holding the lunge line

Lungeing Equipment

If properly done, lungeing can enhance the training and development of the horse and the rider. When lungeing the horse, you will need additional equipment, including the following: The "lungeing caveson," which looks like a padded noseband. The lungeing caveson fits over the snaffle bridle and should be adjusted so that it is snug. It is important to note that the lungeing caveson should not fit too tight or too loose. If it is too tight it can interfere with the horse's breathing and if it is too loose it may injure or rub parts of the horse's face while you are lungeing.

The "lunge line" should be about 30 feet long and made of canvas or nylon webbing. At one end of the lunge line there is a buckle or snap that attaches to the middle of the caveson and at the other end there is a small loop that is held while lungeing. Please remember while lungeing never to wrap the lunge line around your hand, but hold the extra line in neat loops that can be released easily in case of trouble.

The "lunge whip" is a training aid that helps push the horse forward while on the lunge line and should not be used as a means of punishment. The horse should not be frightened of the whip. The whip and the lash should be long enough to reach the horse when he is on the circle. The whip is an aid that will help encourage the horse to move. When lungeing the horse, the whip is held in the hand opposite the direction the horse is going. If the horse is being lunged to the right, the lunge whip will be carried in the rider or trainer's left hand. The lunge whip will be pointed toward the rear of the horse and should never be swung around high in the air.

The "side reins" are introduced and used only after the horse has learned to go forward in a relaxed manner and is obedient in his transitions at the walk, trot, and canter. The side reins are leather straps with elastic or rubber inserts which are attached to the snaffle bit at one end and to the girth at the other end. The side reins should be long enough so that the horse can relax and lower his head while being lunged. Side reins aid the horse in making contact with the bit. It should be stressed that side reins are not used to force the horse's head into position. This is also true about the rider's hands. They should not be used to force the horse's head into position.

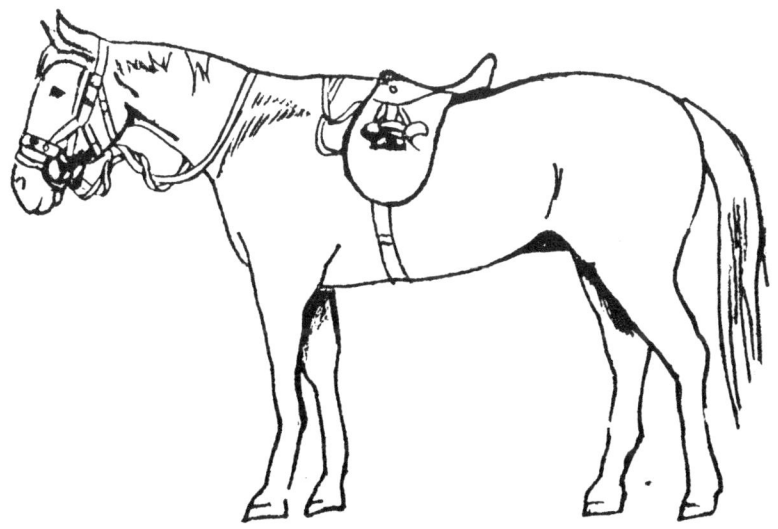

Equipment for lungeing

Lungeing over Cavalletti

A cavalletti is described as a low, movable rail or pole. It should be eight to twelve feet long and four to twelve inches high. The main objective for working over cavalletti is to improve the horse's balance, suppleness, impulse, and rhythm at the walk and trot. If properly done, lungeing over cavalletti can enhance the total training program of the horse and rider.

When using cavalletti you should have the rails placed at a distance of 4 to 5 feet away from each other. What will determine the distance of separation between cavalletti is the length of stride of the horse. If while going over the cavalletti the horse's stride seems short, it may be that the rails are too close to each other. On the other hand, if the horse cannot reach the next pole, it may be that the cavalletti are too far apart.

Before introducing the horse to the cavalletti, the side reins should be removed and the riding reins should be twisted and secured to the throat-latch. Next, lead the horse over the cavalletti and, after the horse is walking over them, in a calm, relaxed manner try lungeing him over them. In a short time the

43

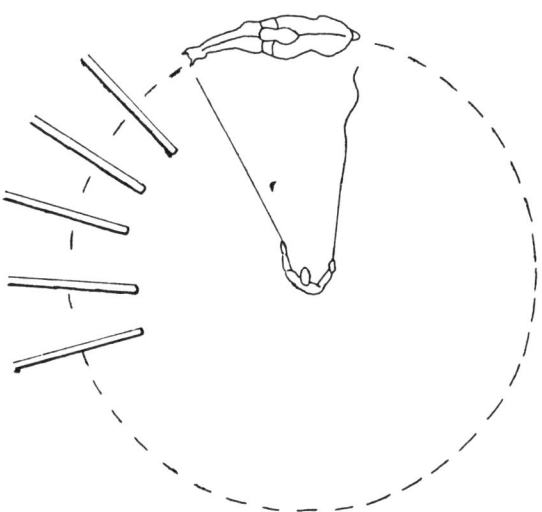

Lungeing over cavalletti

horse will gain confidence and start to lower and stretch his head and neck. While riding over cavalletti, the horse will also round the muscles of the back and improve the engagement of the hindquarters.

Later, as the horse develops his gymnastic abilities over the cavalletti, combinations of cavalletti and jumps can be introduced. Once the horse is working well at the walk, trot, and canter on the lunge line, the rider can adjust the saddle and mount the horse. Before mounting the horse, the rider should always check the girth to see if it is loose. Often, when tightening the girth in the stable area, the horse will expand his rib cage so that the girth may seem tight. But later, when the horse relaxes and is exercised, the saddle may become loose, so be sure to examine the tightness of the girth. To adjust the saddle, walk to the left side of the horse. Lift the saddle flaps and tighten the two straps of the girth and billets. You may find that the saddle can be adjusted at least two more notches. To aid in tightening the girth, place your right elbow on your hip and push your arm up with your hip. This will give you much more leverage. Also, before mounting, the rider should adjust his stirrup leathers. A rule of thumb for proper stirrup length is that the stirrup straps plus the stirrup irons should be the same length as the distance from the finger tips to the armpits.

With a secure saddle and adjusted stirrups, the rider is ready to mount the horse. When mounting, stand close to the left side of the horse facing toward the tail. With your left hand, grasp both reins and place them by the withers, in front of the saddle. Next, turn the stirrup iron toward you with your right hand, and then place your left foot in it. Your right hand will than take hold of the cantle and with your weight on your hands spring

Mounting

Adjusting the stirrups

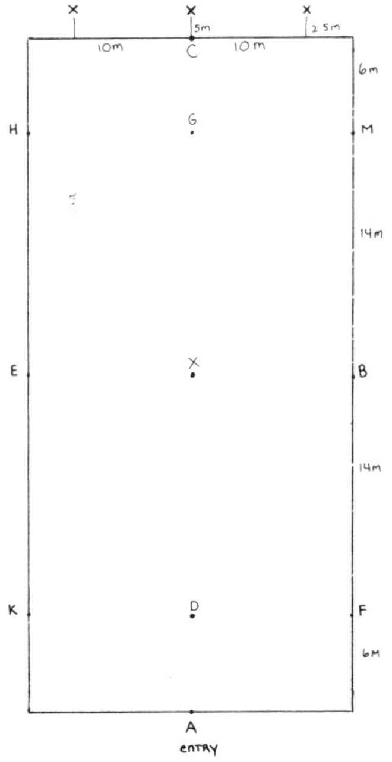

Small dressage area:
20 x 40 meters

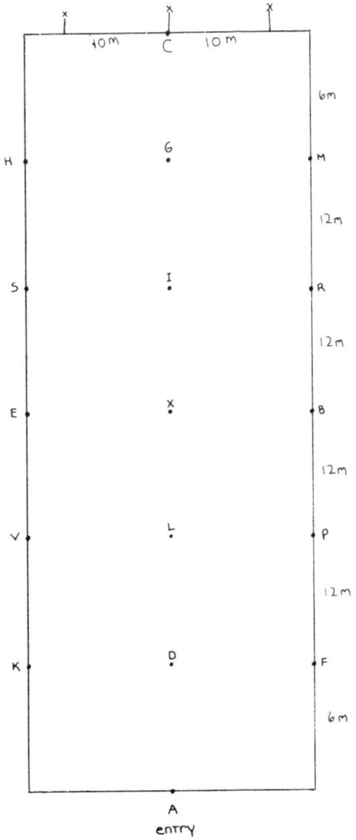

Large dressage area:
20 x 60 meters

Change of the rein across the diagonal

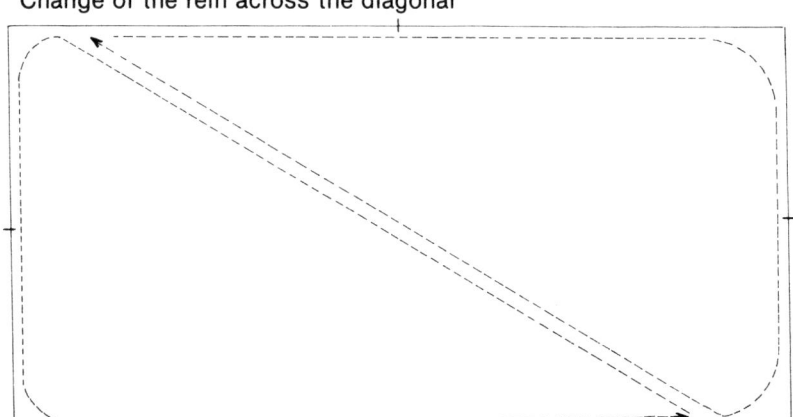

off your right foot and gently place yourself into the saddle. Once the rider is in the saddle, he or she may want to adjust the stirrup lengths or tighten the girth one last time. If the girth is loose it can now be tightened even while in the saddle.

For tightening the girth while in the saddle, always keep a firm grip on the reins. This is a safety measure; if the horse decides to move you will still have control of your mount. Next, move your left leg and stirrup iron behind the girth and, with your thigh holding the saddle flap, reach down and tighten the girth.

Posture and Seat of the Rider

The rider needs a good, balanced driving seat so that the horse can be properly driven forward. To accomplish this the rider should sit in the deepest part of the saddle. The weight of the rider's seat should be evenly distributed as the rider sits erect. The lower back is firmly braced so that it can help drive the horse effectively forward. If the rider's back is hollowed or rounded it will prevent him from properly giving the horse the correct aids.

It is important that the rider's seat be in harmony with the horse's center of gravity. The hips should be relaxed and flexible so that they are resting naturally in the saddle. The rider's hips and shoulders should always be perpendicular to the horse. The thighs will rest on the saddle and should not clamp or pinch the front of the saddle. The knees will be bent and kept flat on the saddle, but should not press too tightly against the saddle or the rider will become stiff. The lower part of the rider's inside leg, not the calf, should gently but steadily touch the horse's sides. The toes should be raised, enabling the heel to be the lowest point of the rider. The lowered heel will give firmness and strength to the leg. When looking at the rider from the side, the instructor should be able to draw an imaginary line through the shoulder, hip, and heel.

The rider's upper arms will lie alongside the rider's body, with the elbows resting near the hips. The forearms should be

Proper seat

in line with the reins and the rider should be able to visually make a straight line from the horse's mouth to the forearms. The hands should be kept slightly above the withers and about a hand's breadth apart. The fists are held upright with the thumbs up and knuckles out. The rider should not be able to see the back of his hands. A good way to remember correct hand position is to pretend that you are holding a rose in a vase. When the knuckles face up, the rose will fall out of the vase. When holding the reins it should also be noted that the fists are closed firmly enough around the reins so that the horse cannot pull the reins from the rider's hand. The reins should not be twisted, and the ends of the reins should lie on the right side of the horse's neck.

48

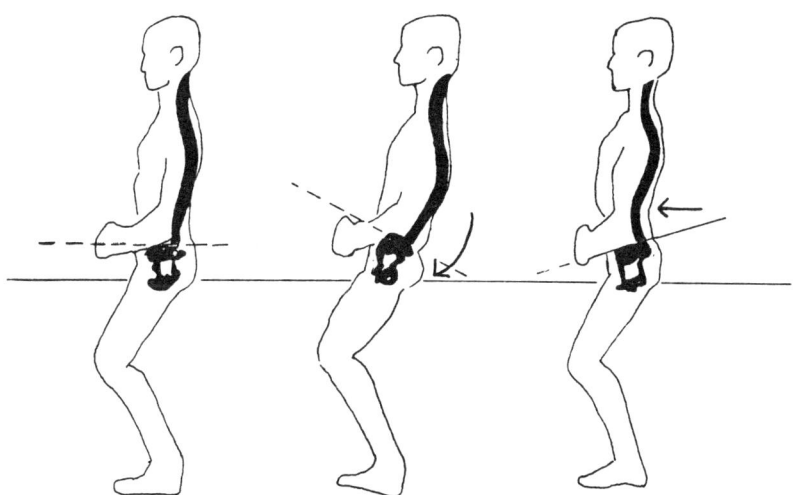

Proper seat

If the rider is carrying a whip, it should be held in the inside hand and should be long enough to be used behind the rider's lower leg. The tapered end of the whip points toward the rear of the horse and rests on the rider's thigh. The tapping of the whip should be with the rider's wrist and should not affect the reins. Any rough motion with the rider's hand will disturb the horse's mouth. Please remember that the whip is used as an aid and as an extension of the rider's leg. The horse should never be made afraid of the whip.

A secure seat is achieved by lots of practice and patience. If the rider or horse is out of shape, the practice and training time should be short at first, maybe 30 minutes, and then gradually increased. To be effective with the horse, the rider should be in shape mentally and physically.

Lungeing the Rider

Lungeing the rider is an ideal way to develop a rider's confidence, relaxation and knowledge. Lungeing enables the rider to obtain a secure, correct, and independent seat. Whether you are just starting to ride or have been riding for years, lungeing

Proper seat on lunge

is a great foundation. A rider can be lunged on the flat or over cavalletti. Before the rider is lunged, the trainer and rider must be sure that the horse is well educated on the lunge line.

The purpose of lungeing the rider is to teach him to maintain a balanced seat while the horse is in motion. Riding without stirrups is an excellent way to improve the rider's position. However, it is recommended that until the rider establishes some security and confidence, the stirrups should be used while lungeing.

When lungeing, the instructor will have complete control over the horse and rider. For this reason it is important that the horse be well schooled. It is very difficult to train and lunge a rider on a "green" or uneducated horse. At first, while riding, the beginner will be stiff and following the horse's motion will be difficult. (Don't despair!) Eventually, with practice, the rider will be able to follow the motion of the horse and urge the horse forward with the leg and seat aids. At the walk, the rider may be instructed to do some gymnastic exercises that will help supple and relax the rider's body.

Once the rider feels confident at the walk, the trot may be introduced. The trot work can be done either by sitting to the horse's motion or by "posting" in time to the horse's rhythm. Sitting to the trot will enable the rider to feel the two time gait and it will also develop the rider's balance in the saddle. Posting the trot will develop the rider's lower body and balance.

Posting at the Trot

The concept of "posting" involves the raising and lowering of the rider's seat in the saddle without disturbing the rhythm of the trot. Looking at the outside fore leg, the rider will notice that the leg reaches forward and then touches down with each step. As the horse's leg is moving forward, the rider rises up from the saddle and as the outside fore leg touches the ground, the rider will be back in the saddle again. The rider's up and down rhythmic motion, in time with the horse's trot, is called "posting to trot."

Once the rider feels confident and relaxed while working at the walk and trot on the lunge line, the canter can be attempted. At the canter the rider will feel a three-beat bounding motion. Practicing the canter on the lunge line will help the rider learn to be relaxed and flexible while going with the horse's motion. With practice and patience, the rider will acquire good balance in the saddle at the walk, trot, and canter. Lungeing the rider on the horse will have improved his confidence and position.

The rider must remember, when he or she is off the lunge line, that communication to the horse must occur through the proper use of the rider's aids. In order for the rider to utilize the proper aids to the horse, the rider must be able to use them independently. To aid in the relaxation, control and independence of the rider's muscles, the following exercises can be carried out on the lunge line while sitting in the saddle:

1. To relax the neck muscles, the rider should allow his head to hang forward and then roll it gently to each side.
2. As the rider's body is maintained in an upright position, the rider can relax the shoulders by first lifting them high or shrugging them and then allowing the shoulders to drop back.
3. If the shoulders and back are stiff, the rider can try the arm-swing exercise. Hold the saddle with one hand and swing the other arm forward until it is parallel with your head. Then let the arm swing down to its original position.
4. For suppling up the waist and developing the legs, the rider can bend over at the waist and touch his toes.
5. Another exercise for the development of the waist and legs is to extend both arms out to the side and while keeping the legs in position, twist at the waist from side to side.

All these exercises will help the rider gain suppleness and confidence, so that he will be able to control the horse when off the lunge line.

The Training Aids

The "training aids" are used for communication between the horse and rider. They are signals designed to influence and make clear what the horse is supposed to do. The what, when, why, and how of the aids must be completely understood if the horse and rider are going to be in total harmony. When the rider's aids are being applied, the rider should remember every horse is different and the application of these aids or signals will vary with each horse. All of the rider's aids must be independent and well coordinated.

Natural and Artificial Aids

The use of the rider's weight, legs, reins, and voice are called the natural aids. The aids can be applied either actively or passively to drive, prevent, yield, or limit.

WEIGHT:

The rider will influence the horse mainly with the leg and weight aids. In using your weight as an aid, the most important thing to remember is to balance your center of gravity over the horse's center of gravity. When giving the aids to the horse, the rider will sit deep in the saddle. The rider's weight aid will cause pressure to travel through his or her seat and into the horse's back. The rider's seat and leg aids will help control the hindquarters. With control of the hinquarters, the horse will go forward. When the horse is moving forward and going into the turn, the rider will place more weight on the inside seat. The rider does not lean into the turns; the shoulder and hips always remain parallel to the horse.

LEGS:

The leg and seat aids influence the horse's hind legs and drive the horse forward into the bit. The leg has two basic placements—at the girth and slightly behind the girth. The rider's inside leg is placed at the girth; this drives the horse and also influences the bend of the horse. The rider's outside leg is placed slightly behind the girth; this drives and controls the horse's haunches when going on the turns, straight, and when doing transition. The inside leg is the leg closest to the bend of the horse and the outside leg refers to the leg away from the bend regardless of the direction in which the horse moves. The legs, working in harmony with each other, will prevent the horse's hindquarters from coming off the straight line or track.

REINS:

The rein aids, in conjunction with the legs and seat, urge the horse in the direction that is desired. They help control and limit the forward driving movement of the horse. However, care should be taken to avoid pulling, hanging or jerking on the horse's mouth.

The forward aids are effectively given only when the horse's hind legs are in motion. Once the leg is on the ground it would be difficult to push the horse foward. Any rein aid that develops into a hanging, pulling or jerking aid will disrupt the forward motion of the horse. The rein aids can either yield, take or hold. When the rider coordinates the use of the outside rein and inside leg it is known as using the rider's "diagonal aids." When the rein and leg aids of the same side are used it is called "unilateral aids." The rein aids do not stop with the hands, but work in combination with the legs and the bracing of the back. The action of the reins is transferred through the hands, shoulder, braced back and rider's seat to the muscles of the horse's back and hindquarters.

It is important to remember that although the rein aids are given to the horse, the transition will always come from the hindquarters through the horse into the bit. The rider's braced back is the centerpiece of all the aids. The technique of bracing the back is an important concept and is one of the few riding techniques that can and should be practiced off the horse. A

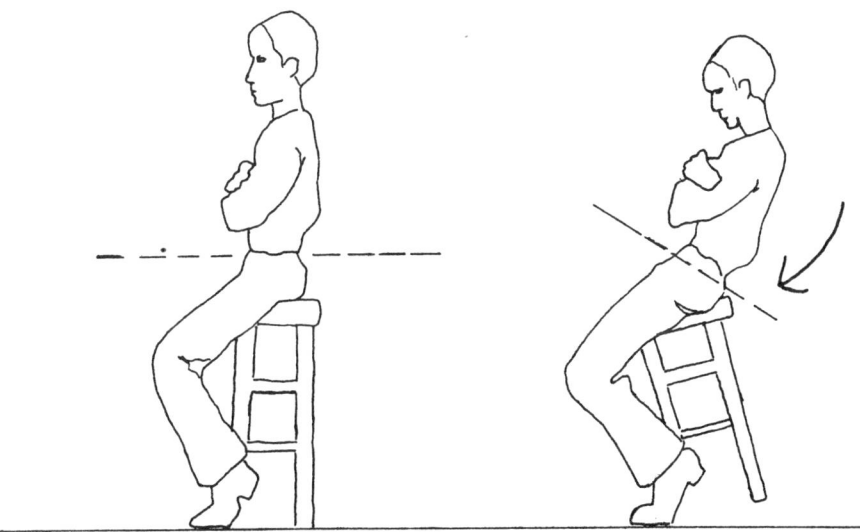

Bracing the back

properly braced back will help control the hindquarters of the horse. One exercise to practice for bracing the back when off the horse is to get a stool and sit with your legs spread slightly apart. Try to tip the stool forward by bracing your back and pushing your seat forward. Make sure your back does not become concave or you will cause the stool to go in the opposite direction.

Getting the feeling of the aids and knowing how to apply them is the single most important concept in riding.

VOICE:

The human voice can be very helpful in the training program of the horse. The animal has excellent hearing. A soft tone will tend to quiet the horse and make him calm, whereas a harsh tone can threaten him and make him nervous. One of the ideal times to teach voice control is when lungeing the horse. The voice commands, in conjunction with the lunge whip, will be helpful in driving the horse forward at the walk, trot and canter.

Likewise, when riding, the voice can be used in conjunction with the other aids as the horse is taught the various movements and transitions so that he will be able to coordinate them. But, it should be noted, the voice is used only as a teaching aid and should never be a substitute for the aids. Overuse of the voice aid will make it an ineffective tool.

Whips and Spurs

The whip and the spurs are used in conjunction with the driving aids. The whip, when used, is placed in the rider's inside hand and is used just behind the rider's leg. The whip should not be used as a method for punishment and the horse should never be made afraid of it

The spurs should be used only by an educated rider who has a clear understanding of the appropriate method of employment. The incorrect use of the spurs can make the horse nervous and may cause him to disregard the forward aid.

Understanding the Aids

The horse must go forward in good rhythm and be supple, balanced and straight while doing turns, changes and transitions. The rider's aids must be independent and well coordinated so that the horse can move with all of his natural freedom. Only then will the horse and rider look and act as one.

The horse should be trained at three phases: on the flat, over jumps, and cross-country. The flat work should be done in a rectangular area that is free of any obstacles. To aid the horse and rider when doing the various movements, dressage letters may be placed on the perimeter of the arena. These letters can be used as reference points when schooling the horse.

Walk Aids

With everything in its place the rider is now ready to ask the horse to walk forward. To start, the rider will make contact with the reins. Normally, when the rider does this the horse will feel for the bit or seek contact with the rider's hands. The rider should never pull at the reins or try to pull the horse's head into position. As the rider makes contact with the reins, both legs will be applied evenly on the girth and with the rider's driving, pushing seat and then yielding hands, the horse will walk forward. Once the horse is in motion, the reins will help control its forward motion. If the horse does not go forward, check for the following aid problems and then try again:

1. Instead of driving with the seat, the rider may have leaned his body forward;
2. the leg and seat aids were not impressive enough for that horse;
3. at the moment the horse walked off, the rider held back on the reins instead of yielding.

If the horse still does not go forward, try all the aids once again and for added support use the whip just behind the inside leg. While working on the flat with the horse, remember that the horse should move forward and stay in good rhythm. The horse should be relaxed, with body stretched, and moving from the hindquarters into the bit with regularity at the gaits.

The rider should be able to feel in his hips whether or not the rhythm is good by the movement of the horse and he should try not to swing from side to side as the horse moves with each step. While walking, the rider will use the reins to steer the horse. The outside rein supports the rider's outside leg which prevents the horse from coming off track. The inside rein aid supports the rider's inside leg and helps bend the horse around the inside, while preventing the horse's hindquarters from falling in. When the rider uses the aids on the same side of the horse this is called "unilateral aid" and when the rider uses the aids of the opposite leg and hand this is called "diagonal aid."

In order for a horse to be straight and well balanced he must first be supple. Being supple means being able to bend laterally and flex longitudinally.

The lateral work involves the ability of the horse to do turns, bending and sideward movement. Longitudinal flexing helps engage the horse's hindquarters which aid in the horse's body, neck and head positions. The longitudinal work involves the speed up, slowing down and the transition from one gait to another including the halt and rein back.

Before the rider can effectively do the lateral and longitudinal exercises which will include the walk, trot, and canter transitions, one more rein aid should be discussed. This rein aid is the "half-halt" or "half-parade." The "half-halt" is used to get the horse's attention and to engage the horse's hindquarter which will help balance the horse. The half-halt is done in conjunction with the seat and legs and must never be a jerking motion with the reins. When the half-halt is properly applied to the horse, it will prepare the horse for the next movement.

Trot Aids

The aids for the trot are similar to the aids for the walk. Then, you might ask, "What tells the horse to trot instead of walk"? The answer is the intensity and the degree in which the aids are being applied. At the trot, the seat and leg aids are more demanding with the driving forward of the horse.

If the rider is developing the trot from the walk the aids have to be clear and decisive, so that the first step the horse takes is really a trotting step. At first the rider will develop the trot from the walk and, after that is mastered, the trot transition can be practiced from the canter or from the halt. Remember, in order for any transition to be clear and decisive, the rider must have a complete understanding and feeling of the aids.

At the trot, the rider can either post or sit to the horse's motion. If the rider sits to the trot, the seat stays securely in the saddle. The rider's back and waist should not bend and move like cooked spaghetti, nor should the rider's back be so stiff that he bounces out of the saddle with each trotting step. The hands at all the gaits are held steady at about three inches above the withers and about three inches apart. They should not interfere with the horse's mouth and should be independent of the seat and legs. The arms are bent at the elbows and placed alongside the rider. The legs are quietly supporting and pushing the horse forward.

If the rider decides to "post to trot," the rider will raise and lower his upper body from the saddle without disturbing the trotting rhythm. At the "posting to trot" the legs and hands maintain the same position as the "sitting to trot." Whether the rider is posting or sitting to the trot, the trot must go forward in good rhythm.

Canter Aids

As with the walk and trot aids, the canter transition must be clear and decisive. The aids for the canter are different than those for the walk and trot. The canter is a three-beat gait and the first beat of the canter is the outside hind leg. To help drive the horse's outside leg forward and to prevent the outside hind leg from coming off track at the canter, the rider will position his outside leg slightly behind the girth. At the moment of the canter depart, the rider's outside rein supports the outside of the horse and the outside leg will be supporting and driving slightly behind the girth, the inside leg is at the girth driving the horse into the canter lead; simultaneously, the inside rein will yield and the rider's seat will push and drive the horse forward. As the horse moves into the canter, the rider's seat must be flexible in order to stay with and follow the motion of the horse. The combination of the outside leg supporting and driving and the inside leg driving with the seat will maintain the horse at the canter.

Until now only the upward transitions have been discussed. But it is even more essential to teach the horse how to stop or "halt." When the rider is asking the horse to "halt," he or she will first give the horse a "half-halt," then steady the reins and with the rider's back, seat and leg aids push the horse into the bit. The most difficult part of any transition or movement is the coordination of the aids and the pressure exerted between the legs, seat and hands. Too much rein and not enough legs and seat or the other way around will not produce the desired effect.

When the horse is at the halt, the driving aids can then relax. At the halt the horse should be standing on all four legs with the weight of the legs evenly distributed beneath it.

When the aids for the halt are applied properly, the rider will be able to feel the halting motion from the hindquarter to the fore. If there is a sensation that the horse is falling on the front legs or that the horse is hanging on the reins, the aids for the halt were given improperly. Don't despair; coordinating all the aids to do what you want when you want is a difficult job. But with practice, time and patience it will come.

When doing the walk, trot and canter transitions, the horse should always seek contact with the bit from the rider's hands. This can be accomplished only when the horse is relaxed, supple, and well balanced. So often the rider is concerned with the horse's head position and tries to force the head into position with incorrect rein aids. With the first stages of training, the horse should go forward with a relaxed neck and long frame. As the horse progresses with his training and is moving freely forward while supple and well balanced, the animal will find the head and neck position that is natural for him. Eventually, with the proper development, the horse will bring the neck up from the withers and there will be an arch from the withers to the horse's poll. The "poll" will be the highest point of the arch as the head stays steadily in the vertical or near-vertical position. When the term "vertical position" is used, it means that the horse's nose is perpendicular to the ground line.

Using the proper aids, the rider should now be able to drive the horse forward in good rhythm at the walk, trot, and canter. But, going forward in good rhythm is not enough for the total development and training of the horse. The horse must be supple and balanced when going straight and while doing the turns, changes and transitions. If the horse can not bend laterally and be flexible longitudinally it will be increasingly difficult if not impossible to keep him balanced and straight.

Developing the Horse

Lateral and Longitudinal Exercises

The lateral and longitudinal exercises will help the horse bend, stretch, relax, flex, and engage and finally become supple. The lateral bending exercises which will be discussed fully in this chapter are the "turns in the corners," "circles," "change through the circles," "figure of eight," "half-circle," "half-circles in reverse," "serpentines" and "leg yielding." Before the bending exercises are discussed, it should first be stressed that none of these movements should be worked in isolation or as a drill, but they should be ridden and practiced as part of the total program. The rider must have the feeling and understanding of the horse. If the horse is stiff on one or both sides, the rider should work on the lateral movements, but should not stay on a particular movement until it is perfectly executed. Perfection is seldom accomplished on any level, and drilling an exercise for an extended length of time will defeat the purpose of the complete training program, which is to teach the horse and rider to move in harmony under all conditions and at all tempos. The rider must therefore have a varied program for all of the different aspects of riding and must employ all of them each time the horse is worked.

RIDING THE CORNER

With the proper use of the aids, the rider will keep the horse straight. When the horse approaches the corner, the rider will give a half-halt with the outside rein and place his outside leg slightly behind the girth. The rider's outside leg supports and prevents the horse's outside leg from coming off the track while on the corner. The outside rein keeps the horse on track, supports the outside of the horse and controls the degree of bend. The inside rein bends the horse around the inside leg and leads him around the corner. The rider's leg and seat drive the horse around the bend. When the horse is going into the corner or on a straight line, the horse's hind leg will move on the same track as the front leg.

Remember, the rider's shoulders should always remain parallel to the horse's shoulder. Therefore the rider must adjust his weight and shoulders to maintain a proper position when riding into the corner. When riding into and out of the corner, the horse should maintain the same tempo. If the horse tries to slow down or lean in and not bend on the corner, the rider can drive with his inside leg and lead the horse back on the track with the outside rein. Coming out of the turn the rider will once again give the horse a half-halt with the outside rein to help the horse balance and straighten.

Let's review the effect of the use of the aids for riding the corner:

1. The outside rein gives a half-halt which will call the horse to attention;
2. The outside rein then supports;
3. The outside leg is placed behind the girth and controls and drives the horse;
4. The inside leg at the girth bends and drives;
5. The inside rein bends the horse;
6. Bracing the seat drives the horse forward;
7. The outside half-halt causes the horse to balance and straighten out of the corner, while the rider continues to drive the horse foward.

CHANGING THE HAND ACROSS THE DIAGONAL

It has already been mentioned that the working area on the flat is a rectangular area and that to assist the rider while doing the various movements, dressage letters can be placed on the perimeter of the arena. This will assist you by fixing points of reference.

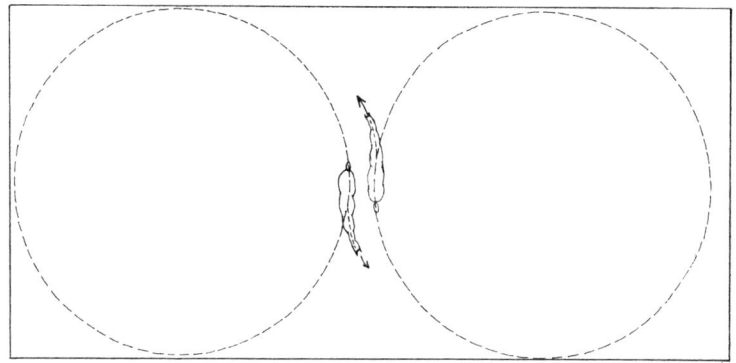

The change of circles

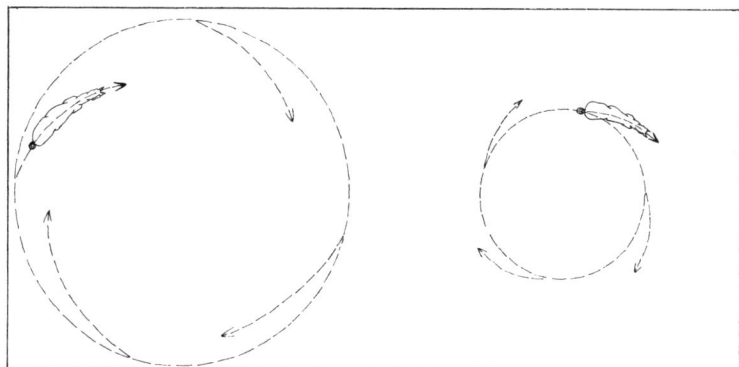

Decreasing and increasing the circle

Figure of eight

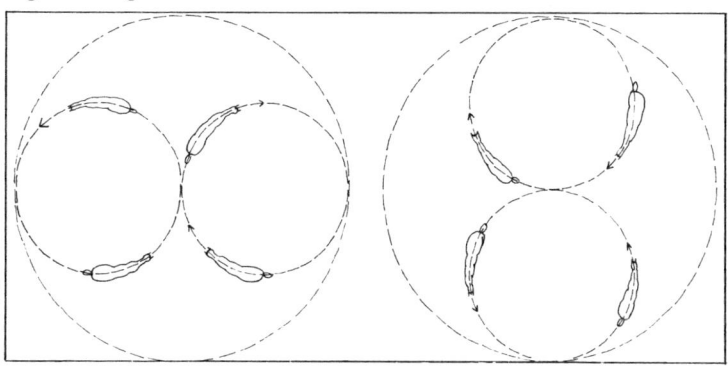

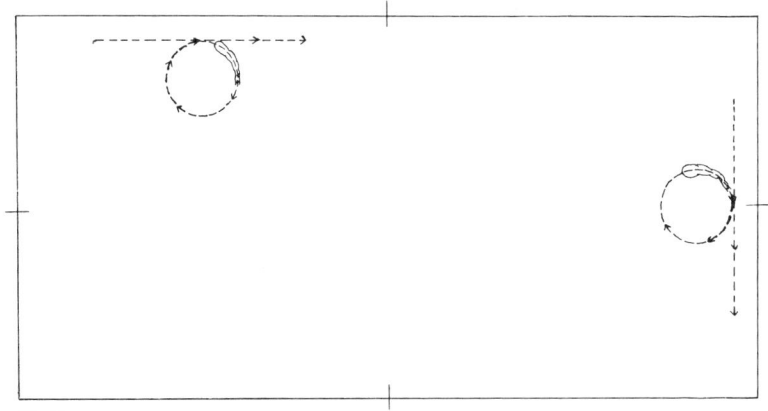

Voltes

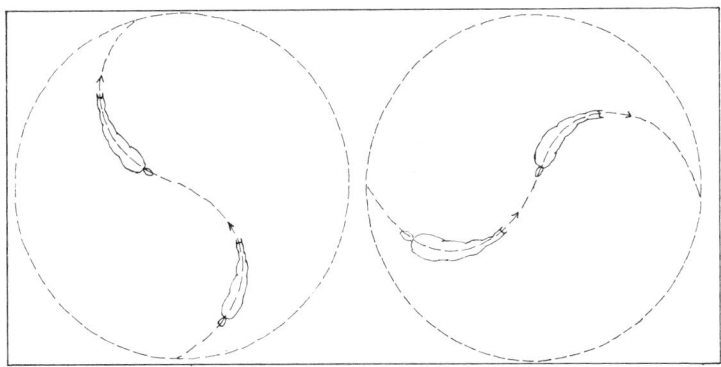

Change through the circle

Half-volte

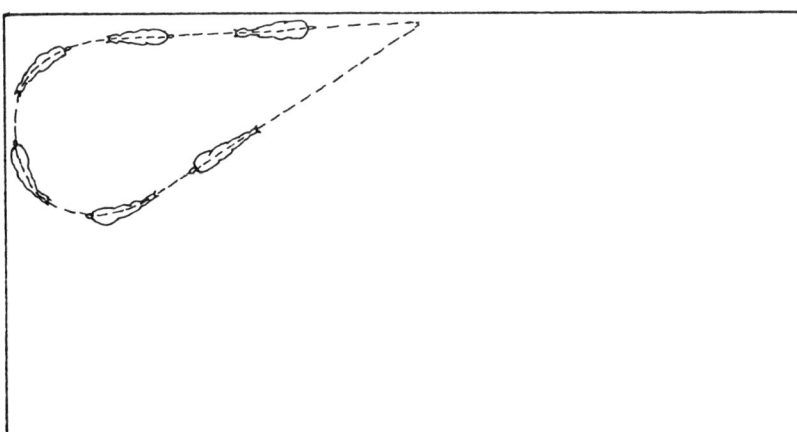

During the making of the circle the horse is bent evenly and continuously from head to tail.

Turn through a corner

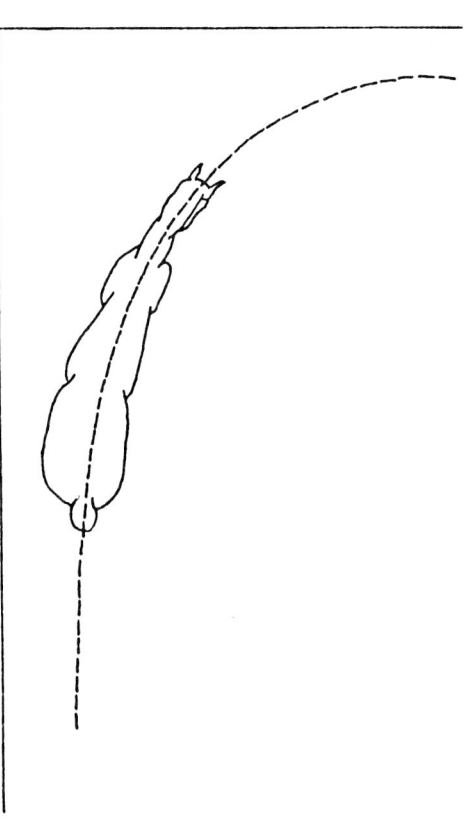

Down the center line

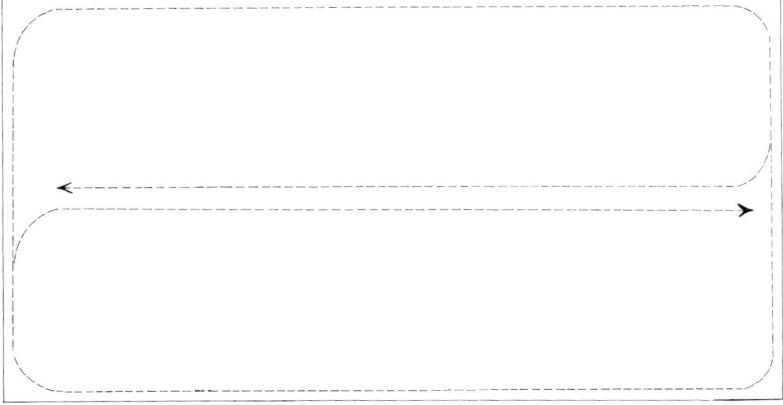

If the rider is working the horse clockwise, the horse and rider are on the right hand and if the rider is working the horse counter-clockwise, they would be going on the left hand. If the rider would like to change the hand, or change the direction while riding in the arena, one way would be to change across the diagonal. Changing across the diagonal means to change direction by creating two triangles from one rectangle. As the rider comes out of the second corner on the short side of the arena, the horse will start the change of hand and ride diagonally across the arena to the opposite changing point. The changing point is six meters or approximately twenty feet from each corner. If you look at the dressage letters of the arena, going to the left the changing points would be at the letters "H" to "F" to "H." Going to the right, the changing points would be "M" to "K" to "M."

Before you direct the horse in a new line, the position of the legs, seat and hands will be changed. When riding to the left, the right leg and rein were the supporting aids and left leg and rein were the bending aids. Now, going to the right the left leg and rein are the supporting aids and the right rein and leg are the bending aids. If you are carrying a whip, when you change direction the whip should be transferred to the new inside hand. When changing the whip from the left to the right hand, first place both reins in the left hand, pull the whip out with the right hand and then take hold with the right rein again. Try to relax. It isn't as difficult as it sounds. When you learn to coordinate the aids, success will come.

Above and on facing page: There is a constant turning, bending motion while the circle is being completed, and during this time the horse relies entirely on the rider's aids.

CIRCLE: DECREASING, INCREASING

"Riding the circle" is one of the important lateral exercises. At first the rider should always practice on the largest circle possible. The practicing circle in the arena is 20 meters (about 66 feet) in diameter. To prepare for the circle, the inside rein bends the horse while the outside rein controls how much the horse will bend. The outside leg is behind the girth, keeping the horse on the track and preventing the hindquarters from swinging out. The inside leg bends the horse and prevents the hindquarters from swinging in. You may have noticed that the aids for the circle are the same as the aids for going into the corner. However, riding the corner has one big advantage and it is that the horse has the added support of the wall or sides of the arena, which help align him. On the other hand, when riding the circle there is a constant turning, bending motion and the horse relies solely on the rider's aids. On the circle the horse is bent evenly and continuously from head to tail. The hind feet go on the same track as the front feet and the horse maintains an even tempo. When the horse is bent properly on the circle, the rider should be able to see just the corner of the horse's inside eye.

If the rider wants to "increase the circle," the inside rein supports the horse while the inside leg pushes the horse into a bigger circle. At the same time the outside rein leads the horse onto the bigger circle and the outside leg drives the horse forward and prevents the hindquarters from going off track.

When "decreasing the circle," the inside rein leads the horse into the smaller circle, the outside rein supports and maintains the horse's position. The outside leg pushes the horse into a smaller circle as the inside leg continues to drive the horse forward.

It is important to remember, when the horse is increasing and decreasing the circle, it should be done gradually and in a spiral motion. Also remember to practice the circle in both directions, so that both sides of the horse can be developed. An easy way to change direction from one circle to another is through the exercise known as the "figure of eight."

FIGURE OF EIGHT

A figure of eight consists of two joined circles of equal sizes. The aids for the figure of eight are the same as for the circle. When practicing the figure of eight, the horse and rider will be on one circle going in one direction; when they reach the center of the arena they will change onto the other circle going in a new direction. At the point where the two circles join, the horse will move straight for two or three steps. When changing from one circle to another the rider will change his leg, seat and hands and the horse will change his bending position. Care should be taken that the horse maintains his tempo and balance when changing the circles. Remember the half-halts when going from one circle to another.

VOLTE

A "volte" is a small circle of 6 meters (approximately 20 feet) and is a very difficult figure for the horse to do properly. Before any work on the small circle is done the horse must be flexible, supple, and well balanced. If the horse is not prepared for the volte he will become stiff.

There are a couple of ways to introduce the volte to the horse. One way is to start with a 20 meter (66 feet) circle and, gradually decreased to half the width of the arena, the circle would be 10 meters (33 feet). If the circle is decreased to a quarter of the width, the circle would be 5 meters. As the circle gradually becomes smaller the horse may try to lean or swing his hindquarters out of the circle. The rider must be sure that his or her outside leg is securely behind the girth and that the rider's seat is erect, which should prevent this.

Overleaf: In the "rein back" the horse is asked to move backwards in a straight line with his diagonally paired legs.

A cross-rail is two rails criss-crossed in the middle and elevated about 18 inches at each end.

Another way to introduce the volte to the horse is by riding into the corner. When riding the corner the horse is already making a half-volte. If the rider completes the second half of the circle from the corner it will be a volte. Remember that a 6 meter circle is a very small circle for the horse and will put quite a bit of strain on his hindquarters. Therefore the rider should not practice more than three or four of them at a time. When riding the circle the horse should maintain his rhythm and tempo. If at any time the horse becomes stiff or shows any sign of discomfort, discontinue the circle for a while and ride the straight line.

CHANGING THE DIRECTION THROUGH THE CIRCLE

While riding on the large circle the rider will direct the horse through it, making an "s" figure. On the first part of the change through the circle, the horse will be bent and going in one direction. On the second part of the change, the horse will be bent and moving in the opposite direction. At the moment the horse changes from one position to another, the rider will give a half-halt to balance him. When performing this exercise the horse and rider should not lean into the bend. After the horse and rider have coordinated the aids for the change through the circle and the horse is making smooth transitions from one bend to another, the "figure of eight on the circle" can be practiced.

FIGURE OF EIGHT ON THE CIRCLE

When doing the "figure of eight on the circle" the rider will make two small joined circles of the same size, within the large circle. The difference between this figure and the large figure of eight is the size of the circle and the degree of bend the horse must achieve. On the large figure of eight, each circle is 20 meters (66 feet) and on the "figure of eight on the circle," each circle is about 10 meters (33 feet). There is always a greater degree of difficulty doing a smaller circle than a larger one. On the "figure of eight through the circle" the horse must do two small circles, each going in a different direction. When riding the circles the rider should make sure that they are round and that each circle finishes up where it started.

As the horse and rider perform the different turns· and changes, the rider will start to feel that the horse bends more easily or feels better on one side than the other. Like people, horses are one-sided or one-handed. They are likely to go better and perform better in one direction than the other. Nevertheless, though it might be easier to ride in one direction than the other, both sides must be ridden equally, so that the horse will develop properly.

HALF-CIRCLE, HALF-VOLTE

The "half-circle, half-volte" is a good suppling exercise that will improve the control of the rider's aids through the horse's body. A half-circle return to the track is another way of changing the direction. If the horse and rider make the half-figure in 10 meters (33 feet), then the figure is called a half-circle. However, if the figure is performed on a 6 meter (20 feet) half-circle, it is called a half-volte. As the horse completes half of the circle, the rider's outside rein will prevent the horse from completing the rest of the circle. The outside rein will lead the horse back to the track on a straight line, while the outside leg returns to the girth and helps with the straightness of the horse.

While in a training program, each of the suppling exercises need not be done every time the horse is worked. But the rider must feel which exercise or combination of exercises will be best for the development of the horse.

SERPENTINE

The horse has now satisfactorily completed the turns into the corner if this book is followed as your guide; change of rein through the diagonal; circle; figure of eight; volte; change of direction through the circle; figure of eight in the circle; and half-circle return to the track. To further aid the horse in developing suppleness, balance and obedience, the "serpentine" can

After the horse is relaxed while going over cavalletti, cross-rails can be set up.

Working over cavalletti and cross-rails will teach the horse and rider
to stay relaxed and balanced.

be introduced. A serpentine is a series of symmetrical curves and loops which will help the horse bend steadily and evenly, while the rider is driving him forward. The serpentine is usually ridden in three or four loops. If the serpentine is performed in three loops, the arena will be divided into three equal loops and if the serpentine is being ridden in four loops, the arena will be divided into four equal loops. It is easy to see that the more loops of the serpentine there are, the more difficult it will be for the horse to perform.

The start of the serpentine is at the middle of the short side, in one end of the arena. The completion point of the serpentine is the middle of the short side at the other end of the arena. Every time the horse and rider cross the center line of the arena the horse will become straight for a step and the rider will give a half-halt to prepare the horse for a new direction and bend.

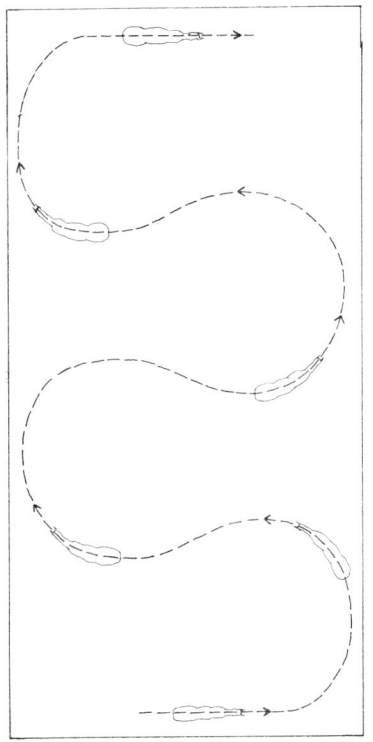

Serpentine

LEG YIELDING

Leg yielding is an exercise that is used in preparation for the lateral two-track movements. When the horse is leg yielding, his inside leg will step forward and over the outside legs. Leg yielding is practiced in order for the horse to understand the effect of the rider's leg pushing the horse sideways. The easiest way to teach a horse leg yielding is to push him diagonally away from the long side of the arena. If the horse and rider are traveling on the right hand (clockwise), on the second corner of the short side, the rider will give the horse a half-halt and bend the horse slightly to the left. When the rider bends the horse to the left the horse will be bent from head to tail and the rider should not see more than the arch of the horse's eye on the bend. To support the bend to the left and the push to the right, the left leg will be used behind the girth. The right rein will lead the horse away from the long side as the right leg is at the girth driv-

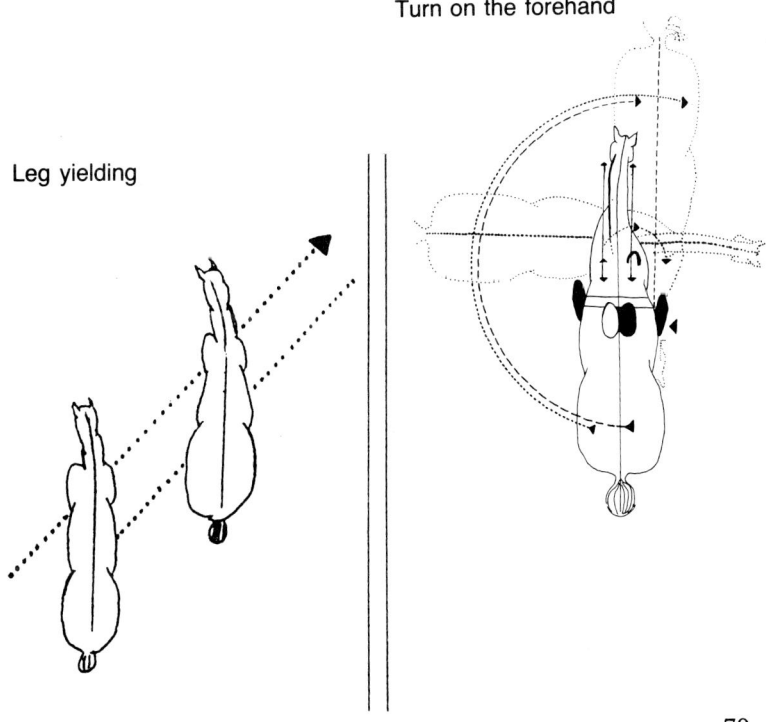

Turn on the forehand

Leg yielding

When approaching the jump, the horse and rider must go forward.

Facing page: On the *take-off* (above) the rider must avoid being left behind. On the take-off and during the jump, the reins will maintain light but yielding contact to the rider's hands and will rest midway up the horse's neck. On the *landing* (below) the rider's seat will maintain its forward position until after the horse lands.

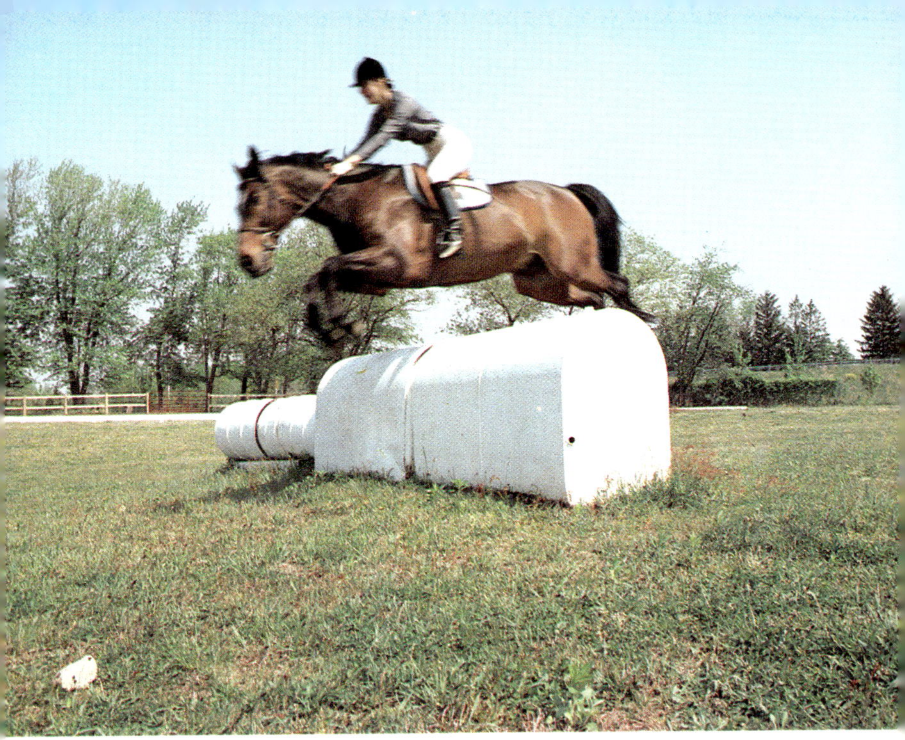

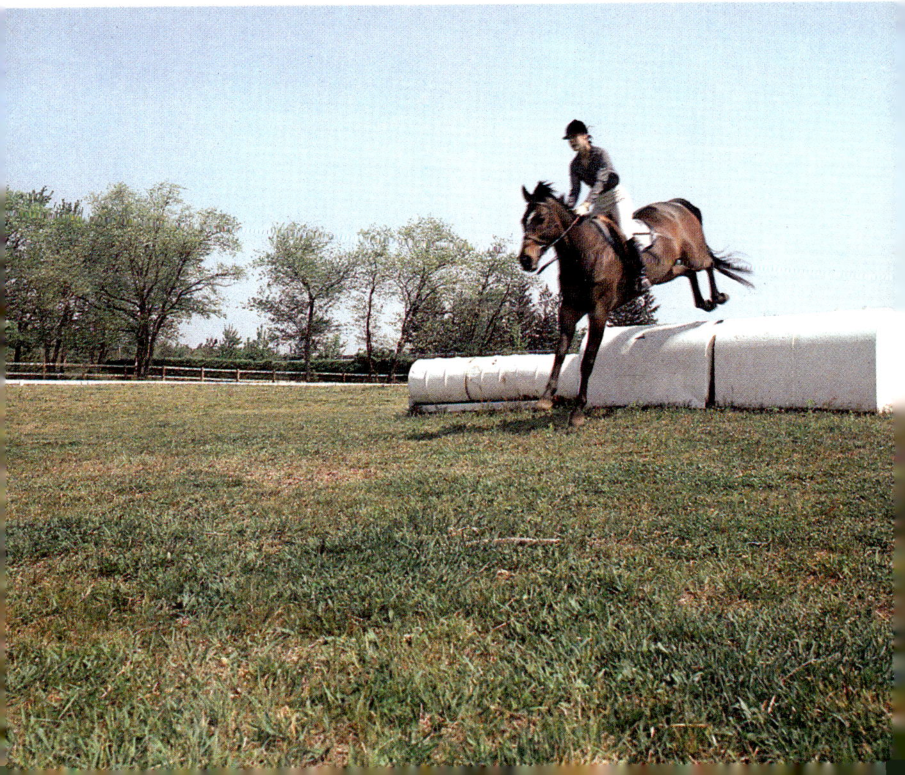

ing the horse forward. If the horse goes too far sideways, the rider should lighten up on the left leg and drive forward more with the right leg. If the horse should lose the forward impulsion the rider should straighten him and go forward; ask for a leg yield another time.

Leg yielding can be executed at the training level where the horse is not yet ready for the collected two-track movements, like the "shoulder-in," "haunches-in," "haunches-out," and "half-pass."

TURN ON THE FOREHAND

The turn on the forehand is another exercise in teaching the horse to yield to the leg. When the horse turns on the forehand, he will move the hind feet on a circular track of 180 degrees around the front leg.

When riding on the left hand, halt the horse on the long side of the arena. The rider must place his outside (right) leg behind the girth and move the horse in a circular motion to the left. The rider's left rein will control the bend of the horse and the rider's left leg at the girth will control the speed at which the horse turns.

When the horse turns on the forehand, the outside forefoot will step in front of and around the inside forefoot, as the hind feet move on a circular track. The rider should make sure that the horse does not pivot on the inside front foot, but steps each time the animal takes a turning motion. If the horse tries to move forward he must be restrained with the outside (right) rein and if the horse wants to step backward, this calls for more drive with the leg aids. When going in the opposite direction the leg and rein aids will be reversed.

TURN ON THE HAUNCHES

The turn on the haunches is a 180 degree turn of the forehand at the walk around the hindfeet. The outside hind leg will make a small circle around the inside hind leg as the inside leg steps and turns with each movement.

82

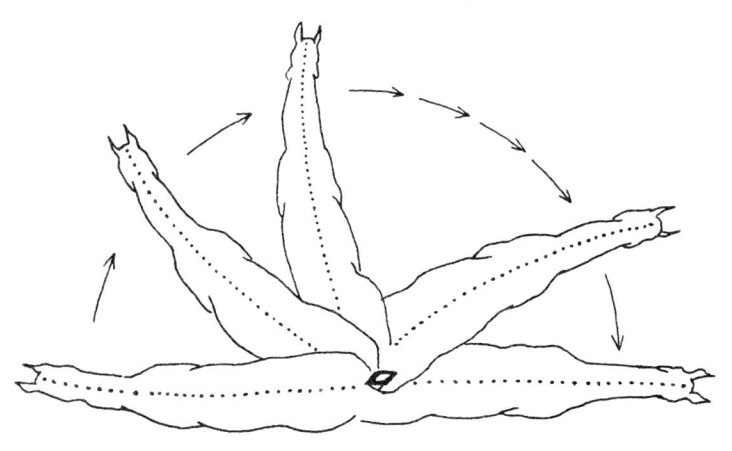

Turn on the hind quarters

When practicing the turn on the haunches, the rider's outside leg will prevent the hindquarters from coming off track and will also push the outside leg forward. The rider's inside leg will control the horse's inside leg and will help maintain the rhythm. While the leg aids are being used step by step, the inside rein will lead the forehand and the outside rein will control the speed of the turn. When practicing this movement, the horse should not lose his rhythm or step backward with the hind feet. Practicing the turn on the haunches will help the horse engage his hindquarters and teach the horse good timing as the beats of the walk are clearly defined.

COUNTER-CANTER

When the horse is able to bend and be positioned easily from one side to the other and still stay straight, the counter-canter can be introduced. Cantering in the left direction on the left lead is called the "true canter" and cantering in the left direction on the right lead is called the "counter-canter." If the rider wants to take the left lead on the left hand and the horse picks up the right lead then the canter is called the "false canter." When ask-

Setting up jumps - a simple figure of eight course.

Facing page: If while riding in the country you suddenly come upon low-lying branches, place the reins in one hand, raise the other arm and brush the twigs away.

ing the horse for the counter-canter, the rider gives the aids in the same way as he would for that lead desired. This means that it does not matter in which direction the horse and rider go. If the rider wants the horse to take the right lead, the aids for the right lead are given the same way: the outside (left) leg is placed behind the girth supporting and driving the outside hind leg; the inside (right) leg at the girth asking for the right canter depart, the outside rein supporting the outside leg and inside rein yielding momentarily at the canter depart.

If the horse is going in the left direction and is on the right lead, when going into the corners and on the circle the horse will be bent to the right. The outside leg (left) will support the hindquarters on the track. Remember that the inside leg is the leg closest to the bend and the outside leg is the leg furthest away from the bend and it does not matter in what direction the horse is going. If the rider finds it difficult to strike off on the counter-canter from the straight line, he can try starting on the true canter and then change the hand (direction) through the diagonal without changing the lead. Remember, the leg position stays the same even though are now going in a different direction, because that lead is still being maintained.

The counter-canter is a good exercise because is helps develop the horse's balance and obedience. It also prepares the horse for the higher level movements like the "flying change."

As has been emphasized previously in the book, the horse must be supple before undertaking strenuous training. Suppling the horse not only refers to lateral bending exercise and movements but also to longitudinal flexing exercises and movements. By working the horse at the longitudinal exercises he will better be able to accept the rider's aids and will learn to move with good balance, rhythm and straightness.

In all movements and exercises, both lateral and longitudinal, the horse will go forward from the impulsion created by the hindquarters. "Impulsion" is a combination of the suppleness in the back, engagement of the hindquarters and, of course, forward movement.

The movements that are involved in longitudinal development are: the transitions from one gait to another; the tempos within the gaits; the halt; the rein back (backing); the take-off; and the highly schooled movements, the "piaffe" (cadenced collected trot on the spot) and the "passafe" (highly collected suspended trot). When the term "collected" or "collections" is used it refers to the contraction of the horse much like in the squeezing of an accordion. The hindquarters will engage well under the horse and the front should become light and elevated. When doing the different gaits or tempos within the gaits, the horse must stay even and regular. The transition upward or downward should be smooth. The rider must utilize the back, seat, leg and rein aids. Some of the ways the aids will be used when doing the transitions are as follows: the back aid will brace; the seat aid will drive; and the leg aid will drive, support, bend and/or push. The rider will also use the rein aids to call attention, balance, bend, yield, and support. When the horse moves in a straight line, the hind feet will track in the front feet and when the horse is turning he will be bent from poll to tail while the hind feet continue to track in the front feet. Before any higher level movements can be attempted or before the horse is asked to perform any collected or extended exercises it must be supple laterally and longitudinally.

BACKING

In the "rein back" the horse is asked to move backwards in a straight line with his diagonal pairs of legs. This means that the right hind leg and left front leg will move back.

From the halt, the rider will initially use both leg aids slightly behind the girth to put the horse into motion. After the horse starts the backing motion the unilateral aids will be incorporated. Taking the rider's right rein and supporting the aid with the rider's right leg, he will ask the horse to move his right hind leg backward. As soon as the right hind leg and left fore leg are in motion, the right hand will yield and the rider's left hand will take more contact on the rein while the left leg supports and

When riding or jumping uphill, lean as far forward as possible and be sure to maintain lower leg and knee contact.

Facing page: When approaching a ditch jump, the rider should get into the jumping position and maintain contact with the reins while trying to feel when the horse is about to take off.

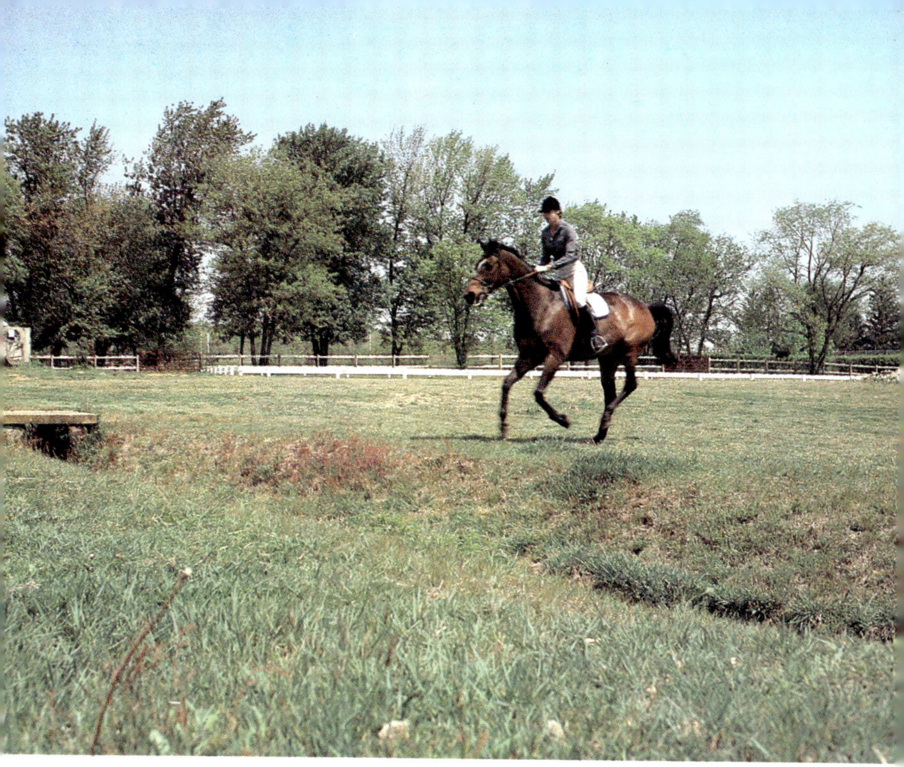

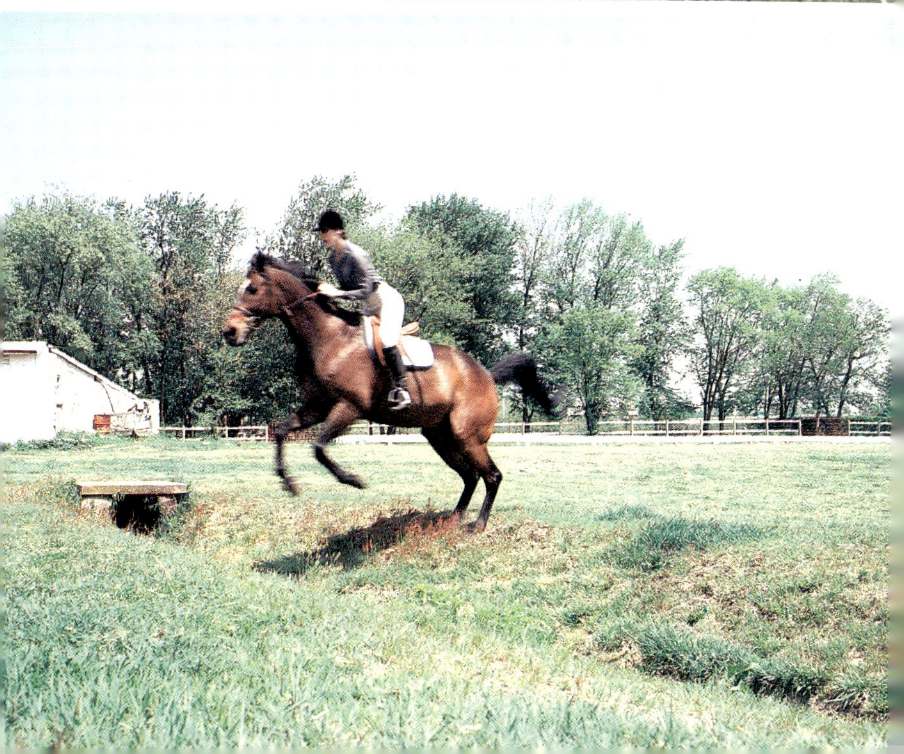

the left hind leg and right fore leg move. If the horse resists the bit or rushes backward, straighten the horse and go forward. Reining back is a very strenuous exercise for the horse and only a few rein back steps should be practiced at a time.

Praise and Punishment

There is a fine line between the use of the aids for education and training on the one hand and punishment for the horse on the other. Before you punish your horse, ask yourself if the horse clearly understood what was expected of him. Sometimes in the course of training the horse may need an impressive aid, but in general horses respond very well to praise and reward. The horse learns and understands through repetition. Therefore it is very important for the rider to have the ability to ride, the time to practice riding and an understanding of both horse and self. Clear long range and short range goals must be established for the horse and rider.

Organization of the Riding Time

The rider should develop his or her own riding program with certain principles in mind. If the rider plans to ride for a hour, then the first five to ten minutes should be used to loosen the muscles and joints of both horse and rider. The horse should always start his training period at the walk. After the horse loosens up at the walk, the rider can ask the horse for the trot and canter work. The physical condition and knowledge of the horse will be a determining factor in deciding what kind of movement and transitions to work on. Whatever turns, changes and transitions are chosen for the training period, the horse must perform them in a relaxed, rhythmical manner. The rider should not drill the horse by doing the same exercises over and over again. This will only lead to boredom for horse and rider. During the training period the rider may decide to introduce a new movement or exercise to further the horse's education.

At the end of the program, the rider should always cool the horse off before bringing him back to the stable area. The rider will achieve this by letting the horse reach and stretch out in a relaxed manner until dry.

Summary

By now, if you have understood and utilized the instructions in this book, you have learned about the horse and rider in general and have achieved a working knowledge about how to saddle and bridle a horse, how to lunge and work over cavalletti, how to train the horse at the various gaits, movements and transitions and, most important, how to effectively use your aids to control the horse.

Until now the horse and rider have only worked on the flat. A complete training and development program for horse and rider is accomplished by work in three phases: on the flat; over jumps; and cross-country. Applying the knowledge and the understanding that you now have, together with a little additional schooling, you will be able to develop a complete training program.

Overleaf:
Sometimes while out in the country the rider might find it necessary to dismount and leave the horse momentarily. When possible, always ask another rider to hold the reins of your horse.

A rider won't always be able to go from the stable directly into the country. When traveling on a road or street, you should always take safety precautions.

After everything is in the trailer or horse van, you should check the vehicle to make sure that it is in ready and working condition.

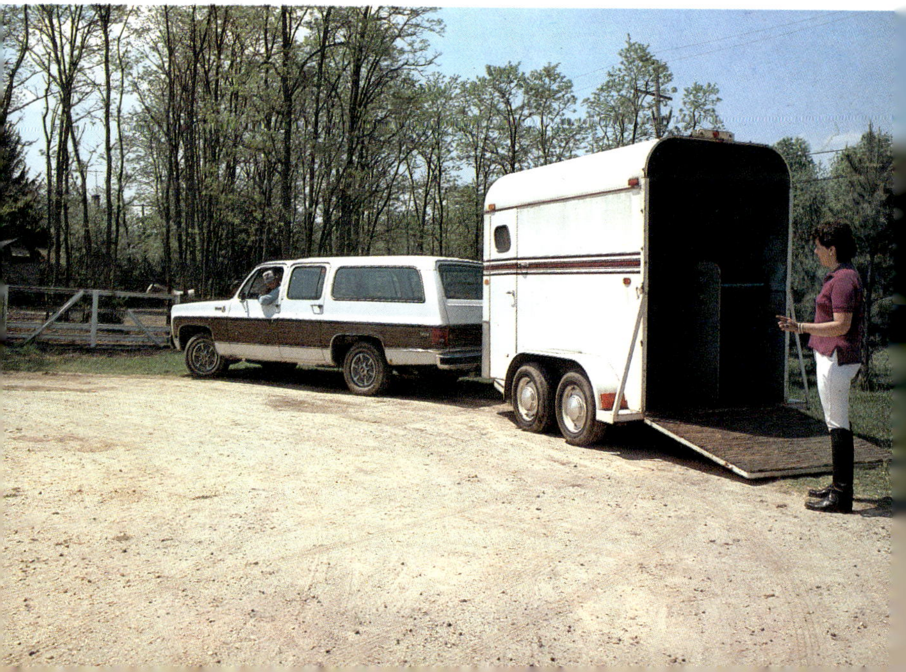

Jumping

Learning to Jump

In order to jump a horse successfully, the rider must use all the knowledge and aids that have been acquired while working on the flat. The aids for the turn, changes, speed-up, slow-down, balancing and bending will all be needed to jump correctly. When developing a jumping training program for horse and rider, the format will basically be the same as the work on the flat. This means that the horse must be developed mentally and physically under a training program comprised of long range and short range goals. When the horse goes forward in a straight and well balanced manner the rider will know that his training is succeeding.

To establish confidence and relaxation in the horse and set a good foundation for jumping, the animal can be lunged over small jumps. The horse has already become accustomed to lungeing over cavalletti on the circle. To prepare for jumping, about five or six cavalletti can be set up approximately four to five feet apart along a straight, long wall. Remember, every horse is unique and will possess different strides at the walk, trot, and canter. When lungeing the horse over the cavalletti, on the straight line, the trainer will walk on the straight line for a few steps and then continue the lungeing circle. This will enable the horse to travel over the cavalletti without being disrupted by the lunge line.

After the horse is relaxed while going over the cavalletti, cross-rails can be set up approximately 9 feet from the last cavalletti. A cross-rail is two rails criss-crossed in the middle and elevated about 18 inches at each end. Working over cavalletti and cross-rails will teach the horse to use his hindquarters and stay relaxed and balanced while maintaining good rhythm at the trot and canter. When the horse learns to negotiate the cavalletti and cross-rail, the jump (cross-rail) can be elevated and the last cavalletti before the cross-rail can be removed. There should now be about 18 feet between the cavalletti and the jump. The horse will then be able to take a canter stride after trotting over the last cavalletti. Eventually the horse will be able to jump higher and in different combinations with confidence.

Riding is a partnership. The rider and horse must learn to jump in harmony. To be in harmony the rider must be in control of himself or herself first and then the horse. The rider will develop his or her own understanding, feelings, rhythm, balance, and ultimately control, by first riding over cavalletti and then cavalletti and cross-rails.

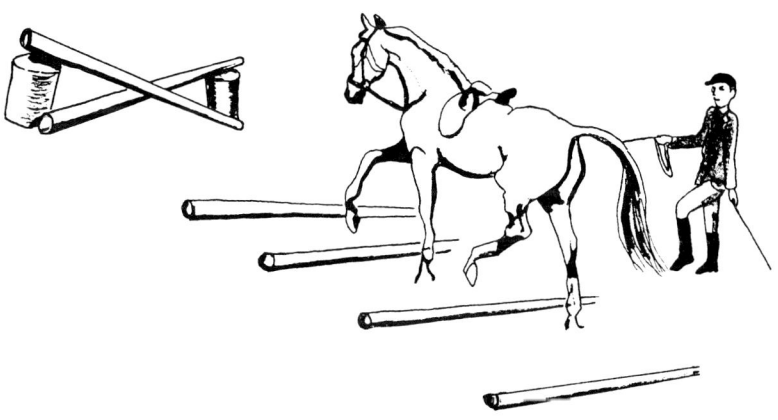

Jumping over cavalletti and cross-rails

Approaching the Jump

Instead of posting to trot over the cavalletti, the rider will now ride in a forward position. The rider will adjust the stirrup leathers two holes shorter so that he or she can get into a correct forward seat. When approaching the jump, the rider's seat will be slightly elevated from the saddle and the upper body will be inclined forward in front of the perpendicular. The rider will securely and evenly grip the sides of the horse with his knees and lower leg, and the toes of the feet or the balls of the

In preparation for a show, the horse and rider should be properly "turned out."

feet will be in the stirrup irons with the heels down. The rider will balance his or her body when going over the jump, mostly with the knees.

When first learning to jump, the rider must make sure that he or she does not interfere with the horse's mouth. The rein aid must not hang or jerk the mouth of the horse when the horse is approaching the jump, at the take off, while jumping or when landing. For this reason, the beginner can and should rest his or her hands on the horse's neck or take hold of the mane when first learning to jump. The arms of the rider will remain bent at the elbows as the hands rest about halfway up the horse's neck. The rider's head will not be looking down and the rider's eyes will be looking ahead. Before approaching the cavalletti, the rider will get into the forward position and after riding over the cavalletti, he/she will maintain this position for another three or four strides. Once the rider has developed a balanced, secure and confident seat, the cavalletti with cross-rails can be introduced. Remember, when learning how to jump, a good foundation is a must. "Slow and easy" is the motto.

When approaching the jump, the horse and rider must go forward. If the rider is timid or apprehensive in any way, the horse will quickly pick up on this and may try to get the upper hand by refusing to jump or by running out of the jump. Running out of the jump means that the horse will try to go to either side of the jump instead of going over it. If and when the horse does refuse to jump, the rider should not become angry or direct any anger at the horse. Nothing has ever been accomplished by a lost temper. The rider should always find the cause of the refusal or run out and most likely the fault will lay with the rider for his or her failure to employ the correct aids or seat. Some frequent problems are the following: The rider hangs or pulls on the horse's mouth; the rider's hands are fixed so the horse cannot stretch his head and neck; the rider did not drive the horse into the jump with enough impulsion and rhythm. However, if the refusal was not caused by the rider, but rather by the horse, look for one of the following problems: the horse has not been properly prepared for jumping and doesn't have a clear understanding of what is expected of him; the horse is unsound or lame and does not want to jump. Nevertheless, whether the problem is the rider or the horse, the rider should always try to find the reason for the refusal and try to correct it through logical training.

When approaching the cavalletti and the jump, the horse must be straight and the rider must have control of his or her aids. If the rider is not in balance and the seat is not secure when schooling over jumps, the rider may find himself or herself suddenly hanging on the horse's neck or sitting on the ground. Don't despair. With practice, patience and confidence the rider will soon be going with the motion of the horse while riding over cavalletti and low jumps.

Jumping

After the rider masters the cavalletti and a low jump, the nearest cavalletti to the jump can be removed. Eventually all the cavalletti will be removed. But before this happens more combinations will be added to the jumping program. A second low jump (no higher than 2 feet) can be added about 20 to 24 feet from the jump. What will determine the distance between jumps is the horse's size and its stride. The horse and rider are now being introduced to combinations of jumps, but the height of the jumps should still remain low. The rider should keep in mind that it is not how high you jump but how well. Only through a correct seat can the rider progress properly. The rider should try to evaluate the jump by dividing it into three categories: approach, take-off; and landing. If all the three went well, regardless of height, it was a successful jump.

Take-off

On the take-off, the rider must be sure that he or she is not left behind or that the horse does not jump out from under the rider. As the horse takes off, there will be a sudden increase in speed and at the same time the direction of the horse's movement will shift upward. When this change of speed and direction occurs, the rider will maintain the position of his or her upper body forward and in front of the perpendicular. This will place the rider's center of gravity forward and in harmony with the horse's center of gravity. If the rider is not in the forward position when the horse takes off, the rider will be left behind the motion of the horse. To aid in the support of the rider's seat at the take-off, the knees will press tightly against the saddle and the lower legs will be firmly on the horse's sides. The feet will be securely in the stirrups, with the weight in the rider's heels. On the take-off and while riding over the jump, the reins will maintain light but yielding contact and the rider's hands will rest midway up the horse's neck. If on the take-off or while jumping the rider should lose total contact with the reins she or he shouldn't worry as the rider's balance and secure seat will protect him or her. It is better to lose contact with the reins than to jerk on the horse's mouth with the reins.

If the rider has a problem with maintaining the correct seat on the take-off, in the air or on the landing, then the jumping seat should be reviewed and analyzed. Perhaps while jumping the horse the rider allowed the lower leg to slip back far behind the girth of the horse, lost the timing and the horse's center of gravity or was looking down at the jump instead of straight ahead. Other common errors are rounding the back instead of keeping it flat, leaning forward at the waist instead of from the hips or placing more weight in one stirrup iron than the other instead of balancing the weight equally.

Landing

On the landing, the ankles, knees and arms, which are bracing the different parts of the horse, will act like shock absorbers.

100

The rider's seat will maintain its forward position until after the horse lands. After the horse lands, the rider will place himself gently back into the saddle and continue at the same pace as before.

The cavalletti and the cavalletti with low jumps are used as a foundation for the progressive jumping work. It helps to create rhythm, balance, coordination, and flexibility for the horse, while correctly developing the proper muscles. When the horse is traveling through the air over a jump, its back will round and the head and neck will stretch outward and downward as the legs tuck up close to the body. If the horse does not jump in a rounded manner, but instead jumps straight, the rider will feel a hollow in the horse's back. This means the horse is stiff and unbalanced and needs more preparation, suppling and flexibility training.

Successful training of the horse and rider is always done in a logical progression. The rider must be careful to take the horse one complete step at a time. Progressing too fast can result in insecurity and limit trainability in more difficult exercises. Obviously it is essential for the rider and the horse to develop a strong, secure relationship and, in the process, create a foundation for further progress.

Setting Up Jumps

Until now, the cavalletti and low jumps have been placed in a straight line along the wall or side of the arena and the rider has used the wall as an aid with the jumping. When the rider can successfully jump one, two or even three jumps, spaced at least one non-jumping stride from each other, he is ready for the next step. A non-jumping stride is the stride of the horse when he is not cantering in preparation for a jump. At the canter, the stride is usually 9 to 12 feet and at the trot the stride is normally about 4 to 5 feet. When setting up the jumps, the rider must remember the length of the stride at the gait at which the horse will approach the jump. Failure to do so will make a smooth turn difficult. The distance between the jump at the canter will be greater than the distance between the jump at the trot. For example, after the jump from the trot, the second jump will be set up 18 feet from the first. This will give the rider one non-jumping stride between jumps. When approaching a jump from the canter, however, the distance from the first and second jump, with one non-jumping stride, will be approximately 24 feet. A jump is measured from the front of one jump to the back of another. Ultimately the distance between jumps will be based upon the stride of the horse and the height of the jump.

Turns and Lines

When the rider can effectively control the horse while jumping on the diagonal or middle line, a jumping course of a simple figure of eight with jumps on each diagonal and on each long side can be introduced. This will give the rider experience in the turns on the circle and changes of direction through the circle while jumping.

It may be difficult for the rider, when approaching a jump, to maintain a visual line for where the horse and rider are and where they want to be. The rider should always be looking to the next point. Ideally, if the rider is on a circle, coming out of the circle to the jump, the rider should make an imaginary line through each jump. This line should divide each jump into equal parts. Also, when approaching the jump, there should be no zig-zagging. The rider should also take special care not to over-shoot the jump. If it is over-shot, then the rider will have to give the horse extra aids to get back to the center line. This could be confusing for the horse and may interfere with his next jump. When the horse and rider are approaching the jump, all corrections should be given to the horse three strides before the jump. The last three strides allow the horse to make adjustments, so that he can take the jump safely. The rider does not tell the horse when to jump. Attempting to do so will only disturb the animal's rhythm and balance. The rider's main objective is to keep the horse driving forward.

The knowledge, understanding and ability that have been acquired by the rider will make him confident that he can control the horse on the flat, over jumps or riding in the country. From time to time the rider may come upon a difficult situation in the training program. If such a time arises, he must remember not to get angry. There is no place in the training program of the horse for a trainer with uncontrolled emotions. When a difficult situation arises, such as a refusal to jump or not wanting to pick up the correct lead, the rider should go back to the basics and consider the following possible areas of error: the horse did not understand what was expected of him; the horse and/or rider has not been properly developed; or, perhaps the rider has rushed the training program and the horse was not yet comfortable with the exercise.

The horse and rider must be comfortable and confident in every step of their training. Only then can it be said that the rider has correctly developed a systematic and methodical training program. Whether riding on the flat, over jumps or out in the country, the horse should be laterally and longitudinally flexible and the horse should respond quickly and obediently to the rider's aids.

Behind the bit

Above the bit

Riding in the Country

Riding in the country is probably the most relaxing and enjoyable part of the training and riding program. When riding in the country, a fresh, natural world will be presented to horse and rider.

The horse and rider have worked diligently for some time, developing physically and mentally, gathering knowledge, understanding and producing a special bond between them. The rider is now capable of controlling the horse and effectively influencing him with his aids on the flat and over jumps. Ideally, the rider should be able to direct the horse forward, keeping good rhythm and balance and moving straight while doing turns, changes and transition either on the flat or over jumps. Only at this stage should the rider venture out to experience the country ride.

Safety
To assure that the horse and rider have a safe and enjoyable time some simple safety precautions should be practiced. Always check the horse's tack before going in the country. If it is worn or dried out anywhere, replace it. Check the horse's shoes to see if they are loose. If one of the shoes is loose, don't ride him but wait until a blacksmith can fix it. In the country the horse is likely to encounter rocks and limbs which can cause severe damage. Remember, "no foot no horse." The rider should wear protective and comfortable clothing including a hard hat or helmet. When there are two or more horses in the group, it is good practice that they stay at least two horse-lengths away from each other. Riding side by side may be all right at the walk and when the path is wide enough to permit it, but it can and will

cause problems at the trot and canter. Some horses do not like another horse next to or directly behind them and occasionally may kick out. The rider should also be aware of any behavioral problems that the horse may have and be sure the other riders are aware of them also. Maintain your distance from the horse in front of you and keep your horse under control. If you should lose control of your horse, don't panic. Try to find an area where you can circle your horse and regain control. Thank heavens for all those hours on the circle! The horses and riders should never race. This is only looking for trouble. If you are directly behind a horse and the horse in front of you stumbles or falls, it would be very hard to avoid being part of the accident. Never overtake the rider in front of you. This means do not pass the horse and rider in front unless he or she is aware of it and in control of the horse.

Riding in the country will quickly answer the question, "Does the rider have a true understanding of the aids and can the rider use the acquired knowledge effectively in influencing the horse when in unfamiliar surroundings?" In the country everything will seem different and the rider will constantly be presented with new challenges. He or she will need to know how to maneuver through the woods, over fields, streams, puddles and unexpected jumps. The rider should always be prepared for the unexpected and for this reason the horse and rider should always be accompanied by at least one other horse and rider.

When first starting out of the stable, remember that the muscles of the horse and rider should be loosened up properly. Please, don't rush the warm-up. The horse could pull a muscle and be incapacitated for months. Take your time; relax and be confident.

When riding in the country, the stirrup lengths will be the same as when jumping. If the rider has been doing flat work before going in the country, remember to shorten the stirrups two or three notches. This is done in case the rider needs to make an occasional jump and will require more knee and lower leg control. Once in the country, the rider may feel that the horse is stronger or that it has more impulsion, more engagement from the hindquarters, than before. Perhaps the rider may want to take advantage of this new-found impulsion to further develop the different tempos at each gait.

Developing the Gaits

When riding at the different gaits, changing the horse's tempo will teach the horse to change his head, neck, body position, and stride. The horse's stride is the distance between his front feet and hind feet while in motion. This means that the extended gaits will cover more ground than the working gaits. By changing the tempo, the stride of the horse will either lengthen or shorten. However, when trying to develop different tempos within the gait, remember that the horse must be taught to maintain his rhythm and balance. If the rider asks the horse to lengthen the stride at the trot, then the horse should do just that. The horse's steps should not become rushed or uneven. Sometimes, when the horse is being asked for a stronger pace or tempo, the horse may decide to go into the next gait. An example of this would be if the rider asked the horse to lengthen the trot, and the horse loses his balance and rushes into the canter. If this should happen, bring the horse back down to a trot, using the proper aids. Remember, the rider must *always* be in control.

When riding in the country, the rider's seat will be slightly different than when working on the flat. At the trot the rider will post lightly with the horse's motion. This will put less strain on the horse's back than seating to the trot. When the horse is cantering, the rider's upper body will be slightly forward, with the rider's weight balanced on his or her knees and supported by the lower legs. In this forward position, the rider must be clearly able to drive, direct or stop the horse and will need to act and react more quickly in the country than in the school ring.

106

Behavioral Problems

Most likely, assuming you have trained your horse as suggested, whether working in the arena or when riding in the country, your horse will act well behaved and respond to your aids. Nevertheless a horse is occasionally subject to a change in moods. This is most frequently caused by a change in surroundings which causes an unfamiliar reaction. This is especially true when the horse faces the countryside for the first few times. This reaction may take place in several forms. Some of these reactions are listed below.

SHYING

Of all the behavioral problems, "shying" seems to be the most common. "Shying" is the abrupt movement of the horse in one direction or another. A piece of paper blowing in the wind or a dog coming out to greet you may be enough to make your horse shy. For whatever the reason, when and if the horse shies, the rider should try not to become tense. This is something the horse will sense from you and add to the problem. The rider should relax and ride the horse forward.

There are usually two reasons for disobedience; either the horse mentally does not understand what is occurring or there may be a physical problem. If a horse shies all the time or approaches objects with apprehension, call a veterinarian and have the horse's eyes checked. If the problem is not physical, then the horse may not understand what is expected of him or something unexpected may have come into his line of vision. The horse must trust the rider and also his surroundings. A tense, untrusting horse will shy much more quickly than a relaxed one. That is why it is important to have a varied training program and to remain supple and relaxed at all times.

When a horse is shying, he will look at what he is shying at and move the rest of his body away from it. The rider should try not to tighten or hang on with the reins. Instead, the rider should drive the horse forward and bend the horse in the proper direction. It may even be wise to try a "leg yielding." Most of all when a horse does shy, don't overreact; this will only make him more tense and he will probably shy again.

BUCKING

Before a horse can buck, he must first drop his head down. If caught off guard the rider can be easily parted from the horse.

If a horse has been standing in the stall for a few days and the rider takes him out of the stall, slaps a saddle on his back and adjusts the girth tightly, there is a good chance that when the horse is mounted he will buck. Also, some horses have tender, sensitive backs. The rider should be aware of this and, when getting on the horse, be sure to sit lightly in the saddle.

For whatever the cause, bucking is a most undesirable vice and must be corrected quickly, with firm direct action. To correct a horse that is bucking, the rider should first try to raise the animal's head by giving the horse strong, lifting rein aids and, at the same time, put the rider's seat deep in the saddle and drive forward with bracing back and strong leg aids.

REARING

Of all the behavioral problems, rearing is the most serious and dangerous. The danger with a horse rearing is that as he is rearing, he may lose his balance and fall, perhaps on top of you. If a horse is a chronic rearer, stay clear of him. He is definitely not the horse for you.

Sometimes the horse's rearing may be the result of something other than a behavioral defect. Perhaps a tree limb has fallen in front of him, or maybe the riding aids are unclear and the hand aids are pulling back too much as the leg and seat aids are driving forward. Whatever the reason, when a horse is rearing he is not going forward but standing still and elevating the front legs. Therefore to solve the problem the rider must get the horse moving forward again. This is done by carefully not hanging on to the reins, but instead yielding with both reins, driving the horse forward with your leg and seat aids and then steering the horse to the left or right with the reins.

EVADING THE AIDS: ACCEPTS THE BIT; ABOVE THE BIT; BEHIND THE BIT

Not all behavioral problems are as obvious and serious as shying, rearing or bucking. Some problems came from an evasion of the rider's aids, but can be equally annoying and can result in a rider out of control. Some of the evasive antics that a horse can exhibit are: going above the bit with his head, going behind the bit, ignoring the rider's leg aids, pushing or leaning to one side and refusing to go in the desired gait.

When a horse "accepts the bit," he will make contact with the rider's hands in such a way that the rider's aids will be effective from the horse's hindquarters to the mouth. The horse will travel in a relaxed, supple and well balanced manner.

When the horse is "above the bit," the horse's head is above the perpendicular of the ground and the horse will not be supple laterally or longitudinally. The neck, back and hindquarters will be stiff and the horse will try to evade the rider's aids. The rider must teach the horse to take contact with the bit by doing bending exerises and working on the circle. Remember, never try to force the horse's head down, but take time to teach him properly.

If the horse goes "behind the bit," be sure to drive the horse forward in a longer frame and yield with your hands. Sometimes the horse goes behind the bit because the rider asks for too much collection too soon. Asking for too much, too soon is one of the reasons that the horse stops responding to your leg and seat aids. If you push a horse too fast with his training, he will make you wait and then the rider will have to go back and start all over again retraining the horse.

Good planning, understanding, time and patience will help to prevent many of these behavioral problems. Secure, independent leg, seat and rein aids will help the rider stay in control and work in harmony with the horse.

Ducking under branches

Riding Actively

To aid in the rider's control when the horse and rider are in the country with the other horses, the rider should ride actively. This means always being attentive and responsive with the aids. Even though the horse is at a following distance of at least two "horse-lengths," he will try to do what the horse in front of him is doing. During the course of the ride the horse and rider may want to switch riding positions with the horse and rider in front or behind. Every horse should learn to lead as well as to follow other horses. There are other exercises for practicing control while in the country of which you should be aware. For example, when the horse in front of you rides to the left of an obstacle, like a tree, or pole, ride your horse to the right of it. Occasionally, halt your horse and let the other horses ride away from you. After a few minutes, catch up to the others. This will teach your horse to respond to you and your aids instead of taking instruction from the lead horse.

It again must be emphasized that one of the main objectives is to keep the horse relaxed. A horse is relaxed when he is calm, quiet and confident. When relaxed he does not resist or become stiff in any part of the body and obeys the aids readily and moves forward quietly, no matter what surroundings he may be in.

TWIGS AND BRANCHES

When riding in the country the rider should be constantly aware of the objects lying on the ground or suspended above, along the side or in front of the horse and rider. Sometimes, while riding in the country, twigs and branches may come into the rider's path. If a rider suddenly comes upon some low-lying branches, he should place the rein in one hand, raise the other arm and brush the twigs away from his body. He should not take hold of the twigs and then push them away; when he lets go of them they will snap back and hit the rider that is following behind. If a low-lying branch gets into the rider's way, the rider should bend his upper body forward and lean against the side of the horse's neck. When bending over the horse or when brushing away twigs, be sure to keep your eyes open, so that you can see where you are going and still maintain control of your horse.

WET PLACES

The rider should be extra careful when riding over wet areas like streams or even puddles. Water obstacles can be dangerous. Wet areas may be deeper than expected and can be slippery. If the rider is not familiar with the terrain, slow the horse down and proceed with caution. The rider should not ride where the ground looks swampy or boggy. Even wet, deep fields can get a horse and rider into trouble.

When approaching a puddle or a stream, the horse may become apprehensive or afraid and try to go around the water obstacles or make a quick jump over them. Be prepared to go with your horse, in any direction. Stay in your forward position and be sure to yield and not hang on with your reins. If your horse won't go around the water obstacle, won't go over it and refuses to go through it, don't get upset. First, try urging the horse forward. If he still refuses, try following another horse through it. Lastly, if the first two methods fail, dismount and walk him through it. The rider must be insistent that the horse go through the water obstacle. Once the horse is introduced to the water or sees other horses going through it, he will begin to understand and soon learn to relax while riding through water.

Looking out for twigs

Up-hill

UP HILL, DOWN HILL

A good way to supple and develop the horse's muscles and make his joints flexible is to ride up and down hills. Because the horse may be cautious when going on uneven ground, the rider must be secure with his seat and leg aids, so that he will not interfere with the horse's motion. The rider should obviously try to avoid very steep slopes and climbs.

When riding up hill, lean as far forward as possible and be sure to maintain lower leg and knee contact. One of the mistakes that a rider will make when climbing up hill is to take hold or hang onto the reins. The horse's reins should be loose, so that the animal can move freely forward and not fall backwards. If the rider needs more support and balance in his seat, he should remember to hold the horse's mane.

Down-hill

When climbing down hill, the rider should maintain a forward position with the knees pressed firmly on the saddle, the lower leg securely on the sides of the horse. With a secure seat the rider will be able to direct the hindquarters and prevent them from moving out to one side. As the horse and rider go down hill the rider should be sure to take contact with the reins, so that he will be able to steer and control the horse.

DITCHES

When approaching a ditch jump, the rider should get into the jumping position, maintain contact with the reins and be ready. The rider should try to feel when the horse is about to take off. Because of the type of jump, the horse may try to stand back and leap over it, or he may stop at the ditch and then hop-jump over it. If your horse should take off sooner than expected, be sure to yield with your hands. Even if your body is behind the horse's motion, your hands should not interfere with the motion of the horse. It is important that while jumping, the rider's hands should never jerk the horse in the mouth; doing so can only urge the horse to refuse to jump the next time. If the horse should refuse the ditch jump, try following another horse over it or lead your horse through at perhaps a narrower spot.

The Fall

No one enjoys falling off a horse, but it can and will happen to anyone who rides long enough. In most cases, when a rider does fall from the horse the most serious thing hurt is the rider's pride. However, there is always the chance that when the rider falls off the horse the horse may step or fall on him and then the rider may be seriously hurt. To try and minimize any injury that may come from a fall, the rider should practice these rules:

1. Always wear a hard hat when riding in the country—in fact a hard hat is preferable when riding anytime, but some people tend not to wear one when working on the flat, since they are familiar with the surface and it is less likely to cause the horse to stumble and fall.
2. Check the stirrup leathers to be sure that they can release easily from the saddle in case of a fall.
3. Be sure when riding that only the balls or toes of your feet are in the stirrup irons. That way, if you do fall off the horse, your foot will not get stuck in the irons.
4. If you should fall, try to roll out of the horse's way as soon as you can.
5. If you think you are injured, *do not move.* Remain still and don't let anyone except qualified people move you.

If another rider should fall from his horse, stop your horse as quickly as possible and go to his or her aid. If the rider is not injured, try to catch his mount as soon as possible. Most horses will not run away after the rider falls. Horses tend to be herd-bound. But there is always the exception. If a horse does run away, don't chase after him. This will only make him run more. Wait until the horse is finished running and quietly approach him.

Rest and Conditioning

When it comes to conditioning, the best advice that can be given to a rider is to "know your horse, know your self and plan your ride."

When a rider goes into the country he or she should know what kind of condition the horse is in. If this is the first ride after a long cold winter's rest, then the horse should not be worked long. If the rider plans to take the horse into the country for an hour, he or she should make sure that the gaits are varied and that the walk is the primary step. Later on, as the horse progresses with his conditioning, the gaits can be mostly trot and canter with only 10 to 15 minutes out of every hour set aside for the walk. How long the horse works at each individual gait will depend upon the horse's conditioning and how long the rider plans to ride in the country. Obviously, if the rider works on mostly flat terrain it will not take as much energy as working up and down a hill or over jumps.

If at any time while riding at the trot or canter the horse seems to breathe heavily, the rider should slow the mount down to the walk. The horse should never be allowed to stand still when hot or sweating. The rider should continue to walk the horse until he starts breathing regularly again.

When riding in the woods, someone in the group should know the route. Plan your ride, have an idea of where you want to go and what time you want to be back. It would also be a good idea to let someone in the stable area know your route and schedule. When riding in the country, ride only where you have permission to do so. Never ride on someone else's property without permission. It may seem like a lot of fun to trot through an open field or pasture, but don't do it. Nothing is more upsetting to a farmer than to see foot prints on his crops. Most farmers will give their permission to ride through or around their fields, after they have brought in their last crop for the season.

Sometimes while out in the country the rider might find it necessary to dismount and leave his or her horse momentarily, perhaps to aid another rider or to move something out of the path. However, regardless of the reason, the rider should never leave the horse unattended and should not use the reins to tie the horse to anything. If the horse should shy, the reins and possibly the bridle will get broken and then the rider might have to walk home. Instead, if there is another rider in the group, ask him or her to dismount and hold the reins of your horse.

Roads

Not always will a rider be able to go from the stable directly into the country. Usually at some point in the ride the horse and rider will have to travel on a road or street. If you should have to ride your horse on a paved road, ride him only at a walk, unless your horse has special shoes that will prevent him from slipping or sliding. Trotting or cantering on a hard surface, like macadam, may make the horse's footing unsure and unsafe.

While riding on the road try to stay as close to the shoulder as possible. Always watch out for bottles, broken glass or other litter that may injure your horse. Another problem that the rider should be cautious of is passing cars and other vehicles. Some horses may get nervous and upset as these vehicles pass by, especially if they sound the horn.

If you are in the country and must cross a major road, proceed with caution. Except for the first rider, every horse and rider will halt and face the woods out of which they just emerged. Turning the other horses towards the woods will help them stay relaxed until they can cross the road. After the first rider gives the word that it is safe to cross, every one should walk across the road single file in an orderly manner.

Twilight and Darkness

Sometimes things don't always work according to plan. It's easy when you are riding in the country and enjoying the surroundings to lose track of time. It may pass more quickly than expected and the rider may suddenly realize that the sun is setting. If you should find yourself in this position try not to get upset. Even after the sun sets, you and your companions will have at least another half-hour before it gets too dark to find your way home. However, if you should happen to still be riding when it gets pitch dark, there are a few rules that should be followed.

First, if you must ride on the road, follow in the direction of the traffic, being sure to only walk your horse. However, if possible, move as far away from the road as you can. Second, put the horse or rider with the lightest colors in the rear of the line to increase the group profile. Also, when riding in the woods or open field, ride in single file. However, if there is enough light from the moon to see the way, you may trot with caution. Third, if for any reason it is too dark to find your way, the lead rider should loosen the contact on the horse's reins and let him find the way home for both of you.

Thunder Storms

Most probably, when you do get the opportunity to ride in the country everything will go smoothly and you will have a relaxing, enjoyable time. While in the country, the rider will be faced with many challenges, testing his or her knowledge and ability. Some of the challenges will be created by the horse, some by the rider and some by Mother Nature. One of the unexpected occurrences beyond the horse and rider's control is storms. Some storms may be fun to ride in. But if you find yourself riding in a thunder and lightning storm the rider should seek shelter as soon as possible.

The first thing the rider should remember after hearing the rumbling sounds of thunder or seeing a streak of lightning is to remain calm. Anxiety can very easily be transmitted from rider to horse.

If the horse and rider cannot get to shelter, they should ride into the lowest surrounding area and continue riding homeward. Lightning usually stikes the highest point.

Dismounting

Except for unusual or unexpected happenings, like thunder storms or accidents, the rider should ride the horse home in a quiet, relaxed manner. When the horse returns to the stable area he should not be breathing heavily, feel warm or be sweaty. If, upon returning to the stable, the horse still feels warm, the rider should dismount, loosen the girth a notch or two and continue to walk the horse until the animal is dry and cool.

When the rider is mounting or dismounting, the horse should stand quiet and still. As to the method of dismounting, the rider can do it in one of two ways. The first way is to place both reins in your left hand and support your body by putting the left hand on the withers and the right hand on the pommel of the saddle. The rider will then swing his or her right leg over the back of the horse and place it securely on the ground. When the right leg goes over the horse's back the rider should be careful not to kick the horse with his or her leg. As the rider is getting off the horse, his or her left foot should stay in the stirrup iron until the right foot is on the ground.

The other way to dismount is, with the reins in your left hand, remove both feet from the stirrup irons. Placing the left hand on the horse's neck and the right hand on the pommel of the saddle, the rider will lean forward and swing the right leg high over the horse's back and allow himself or herself to slide down to the ground. One of the advantages to dismounting in this manner is that the left foot cannot get caught in the stirrup iron if the horse should decide to move while dismounting.

Once the rider has dismounted, the girth can be loosened and the stirrup irons can be pushed up in the stirrup straps so the irons do not hit the sides of the horse as you lead him to cool him out. One of the reasons for keeping the saddle on but loosened is to protect the horse's back muscles from the cool or cold air. Another way to protect the horse's back muscles and kidneys while helping him cool out properly is to place a wool absorbent blanket over him. This blanket is called a "cooler" and it allows the horse to cool down slowly.

After the horse is properly cooled, you can place him on the cross-ties with his halter on.

Removing the Bridle and Saddle

Before removing the bridle be sure to unbuckle the throat-latch and nose band. Next, place your left hand on the front of the horse's face just above the nostrils and with your right hand take the head piece of the bridle and slip it over the horse's ears. Be sure to allow the horse to ease the bit out of his mouth. If you rush the bridle off the horse, the bit may get caught in the horse's mouth and the next time you go to remove the bridle, he may give you trouble.

After the bridle is removed but before the reins are taken off, place the halter on the horse. The halter is basically put on like the bridle. Once the halter is on and the horse is on the cross-ties, the saddle may be removed. When unbuckling the girth, the rider should be careful that the buckle on the girth does not hit the horse's front legs. The rider will then take hold of the front of the saddle with his or her left hand and with his or her right hand holding the cantle he or she will slide the saddle off the horse toward himself or herself. The other side of the girth is then unbuckled and placed over the saddle, with the clean side against the saddle. For the moment, the saddle and bridle can be placed on the tack box or stall door so that you can put the finishing touches on the horse.

Before the horse is placed into his stall, he should be thoroughly groomed. All the sweat marks should be removed with a damp sponge and brush and the horse's hooves should be cleaned out once again. If the outside of the horse's feet are dried or cracked, then hoof dressing should be brushed or rubbed on them. The horse is now brushed and cleaned and can be placed in the stall with the stall door securely shut behind him.

Cleaning and Care of the Equipment

Before the rider puts the bridle and saddle away, they should be properly cleaned. To clean the saddle and bridle you will need a few small sponges, towels and rags, a bar of glycerine saddle soap, saddle oil, metal polish, a soft brush and two small pans—one with warm water and the other with oil or soap.

CLEANING THE BRIDLE

First, place the bridle on a hook so that it can hang down freely. Next, unfasten every piece so that all parts can be cleaned. But, before you take the bridle totally apart, be sure that you know the parts of the bridle well enough to put it back together.

After each part is undone, take the glycerine soap and a little warm water and thoroughly soap both sides of all the leather parts. Be careful not to soak the leather with too much water. After rubbing the soap into the leather, wipe the excess soap off with a smooth rag. After the leather pieces are clean, the bit can be washed off with warm water. The buckles that are attached to the leather pieces can now be polished. With the bridle completely cleaned it can be fastened together once again.

If at any time the leather parts of the bridle seem to be hard or dried out, then you should oil them to help make them soft and pliable once again. Be careful to use the oil sparingly.

Not always will every part of the bridle have to be taken apart after a ride with the horse. Using the same cleaning materials, the bridle can be cleaned intact. This is not a complete, thorough cleaning, but it does get the bridle cleaned and inspected every time. While cleaning the bridle, you should inspect it for leather wear, cracking and any signs of the stitching coming apart. It would be very dangerous should this be neglected as it could result in a broken bridle while you are on the horse.

CLEANING THE SADDLE

When cleaning the saddle, first remove all the various parts. The main parts are the girth, girth-guards (which are small pieces of leather covering the girth buckle and billets straps), stirrup leathers and stirrup irons. Next, brush off all dirt or mud from the girth or saddle with a soft brush and then clean the saddle thoroughly with saddle soap. Be sure to clean all of the flaps and the underside of the saddle. If it should appear that the saddle needs to be oiled, oil only the underside. After the saddle is cleaned, the stirrup leathers can be soaped and the stirrup irons polished. Stirrup irons do not need to be polished frequently but should be wiped off after each use. If the girth is not leather but is web or nylon then it should be washed and if the saddle pad is washable then it should be cleaned every time you ride. The saddle pad and girth are the parts that come in closest contact with the horse. If they are dirty or rough, they may cause sores on the horse. With the horse all tucked away for the day and all the equipment cleaned, you can now relax or maybe even sit around with your friends and tell horse stories.

Competition

Not every horse and rider will want to "show." But, if you should decide to do so, much preparation will be needed. "Showing" is a whole new experience. It can be fun and exciting, but also very demanding. Before you decide to show you may want to observe a few horse shows so that you will know what is expected of the horse and rider. Once you have decided to show, you should join one of the many riding organizations. These organizations will give you all of the rules and regulations for showing and they will also give you a list of when and where the shows are scheduled. With the aid of your riding instructor you will be able to decide which shows are for you.

Preparation for Showing

In preparation for a show, the horse and rider should be properly "turned out." This means everything must be "spic and span." The night before the show, the horse should be spotlessly cleaned and properly trimmed. At some shows the horse's mane and tail will be braided and at other shows only the mane. All the horse's equipment should be cleaned and metal parts except for the bit polished.

The rider should have a "tack box" or trunk to store the necessary equipment. The trunk or tack box is usually placed on the horse trailer or horse van. Inside the truck you should be certain to keep the following essentials: first aid kit for horse and rider, which should include instant ice and heat packs, wound dressings, bandages, gauze pads, cotton, scissors, surgical tape, antiseptic salve and powder, liniment, alcohol and safety pins; complete grooming kit, containing different brushes, combs, hoof picks, sponges, hoof dressing, sweat scraper, hoof polish, rags and fly repellent; braiding kit (even though the braiding will probably be done before leaving for the show grounds the rider may need to re-do a few braids at the show) containing rubber bands, yarn, scissors, combs and tape.

When showing in dressage some horses are braided and then white tape is put around each braid. The rider will also need to bring an extra halter and lead line, extra leather and bridle and lungeing equipment if you are planning to lunge the horse before class. The horse will need a hay net filled with hay and a water bucket; he will also need blankets and a cooler depending upon the weather.

After everything is in the trailer or horse van, you should check the vehicle to make sure that it is in ready and working condition. It would be a shame to spend all that time getting the horse and self ready, only to realize the morning of the show that you are out of gas. So make sure you have a full tank of gas and that the lights and brakes are working correctly. Another thing that should be checked, but is often overlooked, is the floor boards in the trailer. They must be sturdy and free from any wood rot.

When connecting the trailer to the car or truck, be sure it is connected properly. The hook-up between car and trailer should be checked again before leaving for the horse show.

Once the trailer and horse are ready for the show, you can then get properly prepared. The night before, you should be sure all of the clothes that are to be worn at the show are clean and fit well. The kind of clothing that will be worn for a show will depend on what type of show you are going to attend. For "Hunt Seat" or "Dressage" shows the following clothing will be necessary: A black or dark brown hard hat or derby; riding jacket, usually dark navy or black; riding breeches that are tan or canary color (however, when riding in dressage shows, white breeches can be worn); blouse or shirt with stock tie or choker collar, riding pin, gloves (either dark brown or black and when riding dressage, white gloves may be worn); the riding boots are usually black, but may also be dark brown.

All colors should be coordinated. For example, you should not wear a brown hard hat with a navy jacket and black boots.

To add the finishing touches to a neat, well groomed rider, your hair should be well kept. If you have long hair, it should be tied back and placed in a hair net. Remember, when competing you are showing off both horse and rider.

The Day of the Show

On the day of the show, the rider will need to get up early enough to clean the horse and prepare him for the ride in the trailer. Some people like to bandage and protect the horse's legs before riding in the trailer. The rider should also take plenty of time to get to the show and get ready. Some horses will need lungeing or extra exercises before the class. How much exercise a horse and rider will need before each class will vary with the particular horse and rider.

After the Show

After showing, the horse must be properly cooled out and then may be given a drink of water. Before the horse and rider leave for the journey back home, the rider should make sure that all equipment and clothing are accounted for and that all ramps, doors and attachments are secure. Once home, the horse should be thoroughly cleaned and brushed and the different parts of the body should be checked for any bumps, lumps, cuts or other injuries. After the horse is completely taken care of and placed back in the stall, fresh water and hay can be given to him. The only thing left for you to do is to clean and sweep out the trailer and place all the equipment back where it belongs.

By this time you will be tired but will also feel a great sense of accomplishment. Knowledge, time, practice and patience have all worked together to create a single working unit of human and horse. To achieve this is the goal of dressage; "horse and rider in harmony."

INDEX